Contents

T0359972

Welcome

Welcome to the 20th edition of *The Good Super Guide*. This is your comprehensive handbook on choosing the best fund to help you reach your retirement goals.

The guide will help you to understand superannuation: where to start when comparing funds, how to keep on top of your account balance, fees, insurance, extra benefits and returns, as well as showcasing the best superannuation providers — all in one place.

The Good Super Guide is published by *Money* magazine, Australia's leading personal finance publication.

Money is owned by the Rainmaker Group, which has been providing data and research on the wealth management industry since 1992.

Rainmaker also publishes the consumer information portal SelectingSuper. SelectingSuper provides understandable and actionable superannuation information, with a range of tools available at selectingsuper.com.au.

Monthly superannuation performance update

SelectingSuper Comparative Report Card

Rainmaker AAA Quality Assessment

Money
CREATING FINANCIAL FREEDOM

The Good Super Guide 20th Edition

Money magazine
Publisher:
Christopher Page

Research Director:
Alex Dunnin

Senior Researchers:
Pooja Antil,
Sanjesh Pinnapola

Technical Researchers:
Roger Marshman,
Fiona Brillantes, Ian Newbert

Sub-editor:
Bob Christensen

Graphic Design:
Shauna Milani

Marketing: Julian Clarkstone

Level 7, 55 Clarence Street,
Sydney, NSW, 2000

Tel: 02 8234 7500

Email: money@moneymag.com.au

Websites:
selectingsuper.com.au
moneymag.com.au

PERSPECTIVES & INFORMATION

Your super is your money. It will grow to be worth more than your home and will most likely become the most valuable thing you will ever own. And because superannuation is both tax-free when you retire (for most people) and is concessionally taxed along the way to help you get there, choosing the right super fund has never been a more important decision.

Rainmaker AAA Quality Ratings

There are lots of superannuation products to choose from, but not all have a Rainmaker AAA Quality Rating.

Rainmaker Information, like *Money* magazine, is a part of the Rainmaker Group of companies. Rainmaker Information's data and research teams monitor the performance, fees, insurance and extra benefits of Australia's superannuation products.

These pages detail Rainmaker Information's top rated super funds. For more information about the Rainmaker AAA Quality Rating, visit rainmaker.com.au.

Funds displaying AAA logos on these pages are those that are supporting you by supporting this guide. When a super fund has a AAA Quality Rating it means they have submitted themselves to a review by Rainmaker Information. Not all funds agree to such reviews, and so if one does, we think it's a good sign that they are serious about you and serious about earning your trust.

 Active Super Accumulation Scheme

 BT Super
BT Super for Life Retirement
BT Super for Life Savings

 AMG Personal Super
AMG Pension

 CareSuper

 smartMonday PRIME

 Christian Super

 Australian Catholic Superannuation-Employer Sponsored Plan

Australian Catholic Superannuation-RetireChoice

 Club Plus Industry Division

 FirstChoice Employer Super

 AvSuper

 Commonwealth Bank Group Super - Accumulate Plus

 Aware Super
Aware Super - Pension
Aware Super - Personal

  Cbus Industry Super

EISS Pension
EISS Super - Personal

 Prime Super (Prime Division)
Prime Super - Income Stream

 Energy Super

 Qsuper Accumulation Account
QSuper Income Account

 Equip MyFuture
Equip Pensions

 REI Super

 Future Super

 Spaceship Super

 GuildPension
GuildSuper
GuildSuper - Personal

 Super SA Income Stream

 HESTA

 Telstra Super
Corporate Plus

 Hostplus

 TWUSUPER

 LGIAsuper Accumulation
LGIAsuper Pension

 UniSuper

 LUCRF Super

 Virgin Money Super
Personal Division

 Maritime Super

 Media Super

You can find the complete list of super funds rated AAA at:
rainmaker.com.au

 Spirit Super

Are you entitled to super?

Are you a young person working in your first job and not sure if you should be receiving superannuation?

If your employer isn't paying you super but you think they should, either ask them what's going on or contact the ATO on toll-free telephone **13 10 20**.

You are eligible to receive employer-paid super if:
- you are over age 18 and earn more than $450 in a calendar month; or
- you are under age 18, earn over $450 per month and work more than 30 hours per week.

If this is you, you should be getting an amount equivalent to 10% of your wage paid into your super fund by your employer at least every three months.

These superannuation entitlement rules apply if you are employed full time, part time or as a casual, a temporary resident or a family member working in your family's business. They apply to domestic workers too, e.g., you are hired to provide in-home help.

Check your pay slip if you aren't sure – details of your superannuation payments will appear on your pay slip or digital payment summary every time you get paid.

Employers that break the rules are liable to penalties:
- they will have to catch up your superannuation payments;
- they will have to pay a penalty that could be up to 100% of the required superannuation payment; and
- they will have to pay an administration charge per employee per quarter.

This is what we technically mean when we talk about the **Superannuation Guarantee Charge**.

Employer-paid default superannuation contributions should be paid into a **MySuper** product.

If you want a second opinion, you should contact the Australian Taxation Office (ATO) on 13 10 20, your preferred super fund or a financial adviser. To find a professional financial adviser near you, please visit our sister service SelectAdviser: **selectadviser.com.au**.

Find your lost inactive super and consolidate

Finding lost super and consolidating it into your current super fund is easy and FREE.

Australians have $4 billion stashed away in lost superannuation accounts and billions more sitting in inactive accounts that they are no longer contributing money to. If any of this is your money you should find and consolidate it into your current "active" superannuation account.

What is lost super?
Your super fund will report you as a lost member if either:
* it has lost contact with you; or
* it has not received any contributions from you in the last 12 months.

Super funds are required to report to the Australian Taxation Office (ATO) twice each year how much they estimate is held in accounts held by lost members and they must transfer the unclaimed super money to the ATO. This money is held in the ATO's **Superannuation Holding Account** until the fund member reclaims it. Money in this account receives interest equivalent to the inflation rate.

Are you inactive?
You are inactive if you have less than $6,000 in your account and you haven't made a contribution in 16 months, you are not signed up for your super fund's insurance offer, haven't changed your investment options or if your fund considers you to be inactive. If you are inactive, your fund is required to transfer your super account balance to the ATO, in the same way that it handles lost super.

Under new laws that came into effect in July 2019, the ATO will try to contact you, and if you have other active superannuation accounts, it will transfer this money into the super account that you currently use (your active account).

Note that these rules about inactive accounts do not apply to members of defined benefit or self-managed super funds.

Consolidating is FREE

Just about every super fund in Australia has a feature on its website that will help you find your lost or inactive superannuation and consolidate it into your main "active" account. This feature should be easy to find on any super fund website. To do this you need to supply your name, tax file number and your contact information. Note that this can be done for FREE – there is no need to pay fees to do this.

How superannuation works

Australia's superannuation system is complex. This guide will walk you through its core elements.

KEY POINTS

- Australia's retirement income system comprises three pillars: the age pension, superannuation savings and supplementary voluntary savings.

- You can contribute a maximum of $27,500 each year into your superannuation account pre-tax. You can contribute another $110,000 after-tax.

- When you contribute to superannuation, this money is added to your accounts and the investment choices you have already selected.

- When you retire you can access your superannuation entitlements as either an income stream or a lump sum.

- Your superannuation retirement benefits are tax-free up to a capped amount of no less than $1.6 million and up to $1.7 million depending on when you first commenced your pension paid from your accumulated benefits. Only income earned on the component above this threshold is taxable.

> You'll find more detail in other chapters. If you need more information or advice, speak to your superannuation fund or financial adviser.

To help Australians to retire with some degree of financial security, successive Australian governments have developed our retirement income system. It is a combination of your age pension, your superannuation savings, and extra savings supplemented by special benefits for lower-income earners.

Three pillars of our retirement system

These core elements comprise what are known as the "three pillars" of Australia's retirement income system.

Pillar 1: A means-tested and publicly funded age pension

If you are older than 65, have retired and satisfy the age pension income and assets tests, you could receive an annual age pension of up $24,838 per year if you are single or up to $37,444 per year for a couple. By 2023 the age at which you may qualify to receive the age pension will have progressively increased to 67 years.

Pillar 2: Superannuation savings

To encourage you to supplement your age pension, Australians can set up a superannuation account, which is a long-term savings account dedicated to holding your retirement savings. Employees are required to contribute (deposit) at least 10% of their salary into their superannuation account, though usually their employer does this on their behalf (via the superannuation guarantee). You are also allowed to contribute extra money into your account and can choose to set up other accounts in addition to the one chosen or used by your employer.

The good news is these superannuation contributions and your account's investment earnings are taxed concessionally at a nominal 15% rather than at your marginal income tax rates. There are generous limits regarding how much you can contribute or receive as tax-free retirement benefits.

Pillar 3: Voluntary extra savings

You can boost your retirement savings by taking advantage of other concessional taxation arrangements, such as negative gearing, capital gains tax concessions or franking credits. Low-income earners are directly subsidised to make extra personal superannuation contributions.

While many people still qualify for the age pension, as superannuation savings grow and increase in importance for more Australians, when people retire they will find they qualify only for the part-rate age pension.

There are four key decisions you should make regarding to your superannuation savings:

1. How you choose your super fund.
2. How you can contribute to superannuation.
3. How your super savings are invested.
4. How you can receive your benefits.

1. How you choose a super fund

Most people are first introduced to superannuation through their employer, who pays their compulsory contributions (currently equivalent to 10% of their annual salary) into their default superannuation fund, unless an employee has nominated another fund. These compulsory contributions are known as the superannuation guarantee (SG).

Compulsory contributions can only be paid into complying superannuation funds that have been authorised by the superannuation regulator, the Australian Prudential Regulation Authority (APRA). If you are eligible for super choice, i.e., you can choose your own super fund, your employer is not allowed to restrict your choice of fund. But it is not your employer's responsibility to make sure you are a member of that fund.

If you're already a member of a super fund, your employer can not force you join their company's default fund. They have to let you use your current super fund. This process is known as "stapling" you to your preferred superannuation fund.

You can make extra voluntary contributions into your default MySuper fund or other funds of your choice. These funds might be industry funds, retail funds or self-managed super funds (SMSF). If you join a fund on your own without going through your employer, you are joining it as an individual personal member.

2. How you can contribute to superannuation

There are several ways to contribute to your superannuation accounts: contributions paid through your employer, personal contributions you make directly, or bonus contributions paid by the government.

Employer contributions

If you are an employee aged 18 years or over, earning more than $450 per month, or under 18 years of age earning above $450 per month and working more than 30 hours per week, you should be receiving SG contributions equivalent to 10% of your base salary or wage. These compulsory employer contributions, which are made on a pre-tax basis, i.e., before income tax has been deducted, must be paid into a complying MySuper product, or another superannuation fund or product that you've chosen.

You can ask also your employer to deduct extra contributions from your salary. These contributions, known as salary sacrifice contributions, are also paid pre-tax.

Personal contributions

If you make additional superannuation contributions on top of your SG and other employer contributions, these are known as personal contributions. These

Insurance cover through your super fund

When you join a MySuper product or any other super fund, you may have to buy a minimum level of insurance cover. This standard cover usually comprises death and total and permanent disability (TPD) cover, although some funds also include income protection cover. The cost and amount of this cover varies depending on your super fund, but in 2021 it was found to average about $6.25 per week and cover you for an average $200,000. Almost all super funds allow you to buy extra insurance and customise your cover. If you are less than 25 years of age, you may not have to purchase this standard cover.

contributions are paid from your net salary, i.e., after income tax has been deducted.

You may be entitled to claim a tax deduction for your personal contributions. If you earn between $41,112 and $56,112 per year, you may be entitled to a special government co-contribution of up to $500.

Concessional contributions (CC)

You can contribute up to $27,500 per year on a pre-tax basis into superannuation regardless of your age and income. This cap includes all contributions paid through your employer or for which you intend to claim a tax deduction. If you contribute more than $27,500 you may have to pay a special tax levy. Contributions paid this way are known as **concessional contributions** because you received a tax concession in association with them.

If you have less than $1.7 million in superannuation, you can contribute up to $110,000 extra per year in additional **non-concessional contributions**. These are contributions for which you receive no tax concession or tax deduction. If you exceed this limit, you have to pay a 47% taxation penalty on the amounts paid above $110,000.

Note: this limit is indexed. If you have more than $1.7 million in superannuation, you are not allowed to make extra non-concessional contributions.

Salary sacrifice

If you want to add to your superannuation you can arrange with your employer to pay or "sacrifice" some part of your salary or wages, before tax is deducted, into your superannuation. This will be a personal contribution you are making in addition to your employer's SG payment of 10% of your base salary or wage.

Salary sacrifice contributions are included in the concessional or before-tax contributions cap along with the SG contributions made by your employer.

As superannuation is generally taxed at 15%, which is lower than personal marginal tax rates, making such contributions means you will have more money going into your superannuation and also potentially reducing your income tax. This is why salary sacrificing into superannuation can be a very tax-effective way to boost your superannuation savings.

Note: For a salary sacrifice to be effective, you must get your employer to agree with you on the amount you wish to have deducted from your before-tax salary or wage prior to the receipt of those monies into your bank account.

Personal deductible contributions

You may also be able to claim a tax deduction for personal contributions that you make to your superannuation fund from your after-tax income, for example, from your bank account.

This option is particularly useful for individuals who are self-employed or whose employer does not allow them to make salary-sacrifice contributions.

Again, these contributions will be treated as concessional or before-tax contributions for which the cap is currently set at $27,500 p.a.

Catch-up concessional contributions

If you (or your employer) don't make concessional contributions up to the cap of $27,500 in a financial year, you may be able to '"catch-up" over the following five-year period.

For example, say your employer makes SG contributions into your superannuation account of $15,000 in a financial year, you could contribute another $12,500, as that's the gap between your current contributions and the $27,500 cap. In the following financial year, say you receive a financial windfall and would like to make concessional contributions, you could contribute your normal annual cap of $27,500 plus the "unused" amount of $12,500 from the previous year, totalling $40,000.

But to be eligible to make catch-up contributions, your superannuation balance must be less than $500,000, and you can only catch-up with "unused" amounts starting from July 1, 2018.

Concessional contribution splitting

Another way to boost your spouse's superannuation balance is via "contribution splitting". You can ask your super fund to transfer up to 85% of your concessional contributions into your spouse's super account. Your superannuation contributions can generally only be split in the financial year immediately after the year in which the contributions were made. To receive a spouse contribution, your spouse must meet the work test if they are between age 67 and 74.

Non-concessional contributions

Non-concessional contributions (NCC) are superannuation contributions you make from after-tax income, for instance, from savings in a bank account. Such contributions can be up to $110,000 per year, but you do not get a tax deduction for making these contributions. If you are self-employed or work on a contractual basis, you may not receive superannuation, so NCCs can be a good way to increase your superannuation savings unless you have not reached the yearly concessional contribution cap.

> For example, Nina is a salaried employee, and her concessional contributions amounted to $20,000 for 2020/21. She contributed $50,000 as an NCC into super. Nina could claim a tax deduction of $7,500 on the NCC amount.

Note: To do this, you have to fill out a "Notice of intent to claim or vary a deduction for personal contributions" form, available from the ATO, and lodge it with your super fund.

NCCs should not be confused with salary sacrifice contributions made by your employer upon your instructions.

The bring-forward rule

The bring-forward rule enables people under age 65 to make up to three years' worth of NCCs to their superannuation in a single income year. Essentially, they are bringing forward their caps and can put up to $330,000 – three times the current $110,000 annual NCC – into their superannuation in a single financial year and not pay additional tax.

Spouse contributions

If your legally recognised spouse earns less than $37,000 per year, you may be able to make a contribution to their superannuation fund on their behalf. "Spouse contributions" count towards the spouse's non-concessional contributions cap for the year. If you contribute $3,000 for your spouse, you could claim the maximum tax offset amount of $540, although this reduces gradually as your spouse's income exceeds $37,000 and completely phases out if they earn more than $40,000.

3. How your super savings are invested

When you contribute to superannuation, the fund invests your money into the capital markets comprising shares, property, bonds, cash, infrastructure and other types of investments.

How your money is specifically invested will depend on which investment options you have selected. For example, if you choose a MySuper product, your money will be invested across a diversified portfolio spanning all major asset class types, although it will be weighted in favour of growth assets such as shares and property.

Similarly, if you have selected, say, investment options explicitly focused on Australian shares, then your superannuation contributions will be used to invest only into Australian shares. Reflecting this, you should carefully consider the investment choices offered by your fund because your superannuation contributions will be linked to these investments.

Explainer – what is your preservation age?

Your preservation age is the minimum age at which you can access your superannuation. Your specific preservation age depends on when you were born. For example, if you were born before July 1, 1960 your preservation age is 55 years. It changes gradually for people born slightly later, up until it reaches 60 years for people born between July 1963 and June 1964. In practical terms, this means that for people who in 2020 are younger than 55 years of age, they won't be able to access their superannuation until they are at least aged 60.

4. How you can receive your benefits

Superannuation is a special-purpose savings scheme designed to support you in retirement. To access your superannuation and begin withdrawing some of your money from your accounts, you need to be older than your **preservation age** and retired or approaching retirement, or have been directly affected by the COVID-19 pandemic. While these complexities can seem confusing, there are nevertheless some core principles to follow:

- you have turned age 65 (even if you haven't retired)
- you have reached your preservation age and retired
- you have reached your preservation age and even though you are still working you qualify to set up a **transition to retirement pension**
- you have lost your job or suffered a large fall in your income due the COVID-19 pandemic.

There are other circumstances in which you may be able to get access to your superannuation, but these are very limited. For example, you have specific medical conditions, are terminally ill, or are facing severe financial hardship (e.g., due the impacts of COVID-19), and you have no other sources of money

available. In these cases you may be able to apply to the ATO to make a formal request for early access to your superannuation. There is also the First Home Super Saver Scheme designed to enable people to use their superannuation to help them save a deposit for their first home.

When you have worked through these options and have decided to begin accessing your super, there are two main ways to do this: set up a superannuation **income stream** or access some or all of your super entitlements as a **lump sum**.

Superannuation income streams

A superannuation income stream is a special superannuation retirement account that allows you to receive regular payments from your super account every week, month or year. These income stream payments are sometimes referred to as superannuation pension payments or annuities. These pay you a regular amount over a set period and meet the minimum annual payments for superannuation income streams – the purposes of these minimums being to ensure that retirees spend a reasonable portion of their retirement savings on themselves and so reduce their reliance on the age pension.

These accounts come in two main forms: account-based pension accounts or a non-account-based income stream accounts. Account-based superannuation income streams operate similarly to regular superannuation fund accounts in that they offer investment choices but are supplemented with withdrawal options. Non account-based income stream accounts are annuities where you pay, say, $200,000 to your account provider and they agree to pay you a set amount each month until your death.

Once you start a pension or annuity, a minimum amount is required to be paid (drawn down) each year. The following table shows the minimum drawdown rates that apply in 2020/21 (the rates were reduced by the government in March 2020 in response to the COVID-19 pandemic).

Superannuation lump sums

A superannuation lump sum retirement benefit is when you withdraw some or all of your superannuation entitlements in a single payment. You may also be able to withdraw your superannuation across several lump sum payments. But you need to be aware that if you withdraw your superannuation as a lump sum, this money will no longer be considered as superannuation, so if you invest it any income it generates may not qualify for concessional tax treatment. That is, income it generates is unlikely to be tax-free.

Superannuation death benefits

If you are a retiree and you die leaving some money in your superannuation account, your super fund will pay the balance to your dependants. If you are still working, your super fund will pay out your balance, including any insurance benefits, to your dependants.

To make this process easier, many superannuation funds have set up what are known as **binding death benefit nominations**, which enable you to stipulate who among your dependants should receive your superannuation benefits. If you have not made such a nomination, the trustee directors of your superannuation fund have to decide who should receive this money.

Minimum drawdowns applying in 2020/21

Age of beneficiary	Annual percentage drawdown
Under 65	2.0%
64-74	2.5%
75-79	3.0%
80-84	3.5%
85-89	4.5%
90-94	5.5%
95 or older	7.0%

How super choice works

The trick to understanding super choice is knowing what it is, and what it isn't.

KEY POINTS

- Super choice means most employees can choose the super fund they want.

- Employers should let their employees choose their fund at least once a year. Super choice forms can be downloaded from the ATO website.

- There are no rules for how employers should choose their company's default fund.

- Employers should only send superannuation contributions to funds registered as complying with the superannuation regulator, the Australian Prudential Regulation Authority (APRA).

Super choice is when your employer allows their employees to choose the MySuper product or super fund they want. You don't have to use the one chosen by someone else like your employer, industrial award or workplace agreement.

Super choice gives employees the option to swap out of the default MySuper product or fund that was chosen for them and go to another MySuper product or fund. But only if you want to. The point is you have a choice.

But equally it doesn't mean employees can choose any super fund you want either. You have to already be a member of the super fund you choose, and it has to be willing to accept your super contributions from your employer. And if an employee decides to exercise their rights under super choice and join a different fund, those super funds aren't allowed to force the employer to become a "participating" or registered employer of that fund.

Does super choice apply to you?

You are eligible for super fund choice, i.e, free to choose your own MySuper product or super fund, if you are:

- employed under a federal award.
- employed under a notional agreement preserving state award (NAPSA).
- employed under an award or industrial agreement that does not need super contributions.
- employed under an enterprise agreement or workplace determination made on or after 1 January 2021.
- not employed under any state award or industrial agreement – this includes contractors who are eligible employees for super purposes.
- not a member of a government-run or private defined benefit super fund, a fund undergoing a merger, or are not on a temporary working visa.

How companies choose their default MySuper product

Under super choice, employers have to ask their employees at least once a year what MySuper product or super fund they would like to have their super contributions sent to. Employees who want to make a super choice must fill in a special ATO form, a copy of which is available on the ATO website. It is illegal for employers to give employees recommendations or advice on superannuation.

Employers – if an employee wants super choice

Employees who want to make a super choice have to fill in a super choice form and provide the following information to their employer:

- a letter from the product or fund confirming that it is a complying fund;
- proof that you are a member of that product or fund; and
- details about how the employer can or should send the superannuation contributions.

MySuper and choice funds

MySuper products are default superannuation products into which employers pay your compulsory SG contributions. But how does MySuper work?

Super choice has been operating in Australia since 2005, meaning that for many years now most employees have been free to choose which super fund they would like their employer-paid contributions sent to.

But because not all employees have a preferred super fund, employers are required to have in place a default super fund for employees who haven't made a fund choice or who aren't interested in making one.

These default funds are normally chosen by the employer, often in consultation with their employees, or they can use the fund endorsed by their industry association or nominated in the industrial awards that sets their employment terms and conditions.

Because many of the nation's employees who use their employer's default super fund keep most of their superannuation in the fund's default investment option, the government has integrated MySuper into these workplace arrangements by stipulating that only MySuper products will be allowed to be default super funds that can accept superannuation guarantee contributions.

MySuper in practice

For the majority of employers and employees who use their default super fund's default investment option and who have that fund's standard insurance cover, MySuper will not impact them much at all. They will simply become a member of that fund's MySuper option, which in most cases was the default investment option they were already using anyway.

All the usual provisions of super fund choice also apply. Because MySuper products are in most cases a specially designated investment option within a regular super fund, they can also have their balance spread across the MySuper option and other investment options offered by the same super fund.

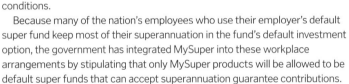

Stapling

When you start a new job, if you're already a member of a MySuper product or superannuation fund, your superannuation contributions will be sent to this fund unless you tell your employee otherwise. This means your new employer can not force you to join the company's default MySuper product.

But if you have never had a superannuation account before, you will need to choose one, or your employer will create an account for you with their default fund. It is your employer's job to check if their new employees have an existing superannuation account.

KEY POINTS

- A MySuper product can be a stand-alone superannuation product or it can be offered as one of the choices contained in a regular super fund.

- Default superannuation guarantee (SG) employer-paid contributions can only be paid into a MySuper product or a fund that has a MySuper option.

- Under the new MySuper "stapling" laws, if you're already a member of a super fund, your new employer must pay superannuation contributions into that fund.

Different types of super funds

Superannuation funds come in different types and market segments. Here we explain what each of these is so you can be sure to join the fund that suits you.

KEY POINTS

- The main types of super funds are workplace, personal and retirement.

- Workplace funds are those you join through your employer.

- Personal funds are those you join as a private individual.

- If a fund is "public offer" it means it is open to the public. All personal funds are public offer but many workplace funds are as well now.

- Retirement funds are those designed specially for people who are retired.

- Self-managed super funds (SMSF) are small private personal funds that individuals can set up.

Now that you understand how MySuper and super choice works, the next question is: which fund should you join? In making this choice, it helps to first understand the different types of super funds and their various market segments.

Modern superannuation started as part of the industrial award system and this meant employers paid most super contributions as part of the superannuation guarantee scheme. It should therefore come as no surprise that most super funds used to be highly involved with employers, rather than work directly with individual members. It should also not surprise you that this led to superannuation funds being very focused on employer administration needs, rather than on individual members.

However, following the introduction of super choice in 2005 and MySuper in 2013, the focus of superannuation funds shifted from being on employers to being much more on the members – people like you.

Using this background, we will now walk through the types of funds that are available:

- **Workplace funds** — super arranged by and through an employer, including MySuper products.
- **Personal funds** — funds members choose on their own as private individuals.
- **Retirement funds** — funds for members who have retired.

Workplace super funds

Workplace super funds are those that are available to employers, whether they are private sector companies, public sector agencies or government departments. A major feature of these workplace funds, including an associated MySuper product, is that because they are able to take advantage of the business volume that comes from combining the superannuation buying power of a large number of employees, they are generally cheaper than personal funds.

When looking at workplace super funds, there are two main ways for an employer to organise them:

- **Employers outsource the fund** – Rather than run their own fund, they use an industry or retail fund. Large employers using retail funds will usually use what are known as corporate master trusts while small employers may use regular personal retail funds known, in this case, as personal master trusts. These terms are described in more detail later in this chapter.

- **Employers can choose to operate their own funds** – If a company runs its own super fund, it is said to run its own "in-house" corporate fund. Examples of big companies doing this are Telstra and Qantas. Federal, state and some local governments also directly sponsor their own super funds, which are used by their own employees, or employees of the government businesses they own and operate.

Personal super funds

Personal super funds are those that are available to individual consumers. Because personal super funds are sold to individual consumers rather than to large-scale workplaces, they will usually charge higher fees than workplace funds. And, because these funds are sold to individuals separately, they are usually accessed through financial advisers, who often have to explain them to their consumer clients while also having to explain how superannuation itself works.

This means that personal super funds have higher sales and cost structures than workplace super funds. Since the financial adviser has to do this one client at a time without the benefits of economies of scale, it can make the process more complex than it is for workplace super funds.

MySuper products are workplace funds because they can only be offered to employees through their employer. Employers are only allowed to pay default superannuation guarantee (SG) contributions into MySuper products, or funds that offer a MySuper product.

Retirement funds

Retirement funds are funds specially designed for members who have retired. These funds can be associated with the fund the member used while they were still in the paid workforce, e.g., they might be a sub-division, or they may be a totally separate fund.

Retirement funds are designed to pay members a regular pension or "income stream" benefit payment, say each month, rather than help you accumulate new superannuation savings. You should also be able to draw down capital for special purposes if needed. Because of these extra requirements, they might have slightly higher fees than other funds.

Retirement funds, because they are designed for a different purpose, tend to have fewer investment choices and do not offer insurance. But they usually have access options for how members can obtain their benefits, e.g., ATM access and links to cash management accounts.

Self-managed super funds

Self-managed super funds (SMSFs) are those where small groups of individual members (six or less) decide to operate their own fund. In technical terms, all the members of an SMSF must be trustees of the fund or they must pay a professional trustee company to provide this service. Anybody can run an SMSF, but because they can often cost several thousand dollars each year to run, they are mostly suited to people with several hundred thousand dollars in superannuation.

Superannuation market segments

Now that you know the different types of super funds, we will explain the various superannuation fund market segments.

In-house corporate super funds

Recall that in-house corporate super funds are operated by an employer sponsor on a "stand alone" basis, meaning the company which employs the members is also the sponsor of the super fund. The fund is usually managed by a board of trustees who are jointly chosen by the employer sponsor and the employees themselves.

In-house corporate super funds operate on a not-for-profit basis, meaning that the trustee company operating the fund does not seek to make a profit from running the fund, and so can often charge members quite low fees. In many cases the sponsoring employer will pay some of the fund's fees directly, meaning that the fund members themselves often benefit from having to pay only marginal fees, if any, to be in the in-house corporate super fund.

Public sector super funds

Public sector super funds, sometimes also called government super funds, are very similar to in-house corporate super funds except that the employer sponsor is the local, state or federal government, or a business enterprise they co-own or operate.

Defined benefit funds are those where your retirement benefit is based on a defined formula that takes into account such factors as your age, length of service and salary at retirement. In defined benefit funds the sponsor of the fund, e.g., the employer or government agency that runs the fund, wears the investment risk, i.e., even if the fund's investment returns are poor they are still required to pay your benefits.

Defined benefit funds are usually part of a broader defined benefit scheme – the fund is just the legal financial investment pool that stores the contributions and through which members receive their benefits.

Defined benefit superannuation is known for being very generous, paying much higher benefits than members could normally afford. This is why most defined benefit schemes are now closed – scheme sponsors can no longer afford them. If you are a member of defined benefit scheme, you should be very wary if someone tries to convince you to leave. HINT: ask yourself why they want you to leave.

These funds are usually managed by a board of trustees who are jointly chosen by the employer sponsor and nominated union(s) as the de facto representatives of the employees themselves.

Public sector funds operate on a not-for-profit basis, meaning the trustee management company operating the fund does not seek to make any profits and so can often charge members quite low fees. Most public sector fund sponsors pay most of the fees for their super funds, and so fund members themselves pay very low fees.

These very low fees are in addition to the very generous levels of superannuation contributions paid by most government employers – many government employees have higher contributions than the basic 10% superannuation guarantee level paid to private sector employees. This can make public sector super funds very attractive compared to other types of super funds.

Adding complexity, some public sector funds have become public offer and now prefer to be known as industry funds.

Industry super funds

Industry super funds are funds operated by parties to industrial awards (usually employer associations and unions) to provide superannuation to people who work in a common industry or group of associated industries. Industry funds are usually managed by a board of trustees who are jointly chosen by the employer sponsors and the associated unions as the de facto representatives of the employees themselves.

These industry funds also operate on a not-for-profit basis, meaning that the trustee company operating the fund does not seek to make any profits, and so can often charge members quite low fees.

Retail super funds

Retail super funds are funds operated by commercial organisations such as banking, insurance, investment management and financial planning groups. This is why they are sometimes called "for profit" funds. They may also be referred to as "master trusts" because the fund operates under what is known as a master trust deed that bundles together the underlying collection of investment options, many of which may be regular managed funds.

Retail funds being known as master trusts is why, if they operate in the workplace sector or as a MySuper product, they may be called a **corporate master trust**. In contrast, a retail super fund that operates in the personal superannuation sector may be referred to as a **personal master trust**.

Lifecycle superannuation products

What are they, how do they work, and should you choose one for your default MySuper investment strategy?

Lifecycle superannuation products are investment choices where the asset allocation is determined by how old the member is or how long they have until they expect to retire. They are becoming very popular as they now make up almost half of all MySuper products. They are favored by not-for-profit and retail super funds alike.

The idea behind lifecycle investments is that when you are young you have a long time until you retire, so you should be comfortable taking more investment risk with the expectation that you will achieve higher investment returns. But as you get older, particularly in the decade leading up to retirement, you become more focused on preserving your capital so you

lower your investment risk by reducing your exposure to growth assets like shares and property. This is done by having more of your superannuation savings switched across into defensive assets like bonds and cash.

In practical terms, this means when you are under age 40 your exposure to growth assets will average almost 90%, before progressively reducing to an average of 53% by the time you are in your 50s. By age 65 when most people retire, the average lifecycle MySuper product has about 45% of its portfolio invested into growth assets. This is illustrated in the chart.

Lifecycle investment asset allocation glidepath 2021

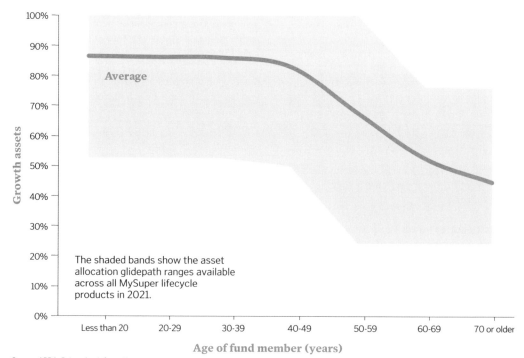

The shaded bands show the asset allocation glidepath ranges available across all MySuper lifecycle products in 2021.

Source: APRA, Rainmaker Information

KEY POINTS

- In lifecycle investments you are assigned an asset allocation based on your age.

- They are designed to insulate older fund members against the impacts of a sudden fall in capital markets when they are approaching retirement.

- The way the asset allocation changes as you get older is known as the lifecycle investment's glidepath trajectory.

Are lifecycle investments safer?

Lower investment risk doesn't come without potential cost. This is because when you choose a lifecycle investment, whereby as you get older more of your account balance is allocated into defensive assets, it means that over your superannuation life your portfolio is more conservatively invested than if you had chosen a traditional single-strategy diversified growth portfolio.

The way this could impact your account balance is that when you are older and have a larger account balance,

the lower expected investment returns delivered from a typical lifecycle superannuation product designed for older people means you will not get the same compound interest boost as fund members invested into a traditional diversified growth portfolio.

As a result, for a lifecycle strategy to pay off, you are in effect betting the investment markets will fall sharply in the years approaching your retirement. How you feel about these investment risks determines whether you should choose to be in a lifecycle investment strategy.

What to look for

There are big variations in asset allocation among lifecycle investment products. As shown in the chart, some have allocations to growth assets as high as traditional single-strategy diversified growth portfolios. But some are very conservative, so by the time you retire you could have less than one-third of your account balance in growth assets. Just as you compare regular MySuper products, you need to also compare lifecycle investment products and be sure they suit your expectations.

Who runs your super fund?

MySuper products and super funds use many different expert advisers. Understanding the different roles they all play will help you make better sense of how a fund operates.

KEY POINTS

- The people who run your fund are called trustees.

- Investment managers look after your fund's investments.

- Trustees often use asset consultants to help them choose which investment managers to use, and to help them decide their investment strategy.

- Specialist fund administration companies help your trustees run the back-end administration of your fund, including its call centre and making sure it complies with all government rules.

Recall that a MySuper product or super fund is nothing more than a savings fund that you invest in during your working life so that by the time you retire you have accumulated enough money to help pay a reasonable lump sum or pension. To understand how good your MySuper product or super fund is likely to be in delivering this, it will help if you understand the main roles people play at a super fund so you can properly judge each person against his or her role. To do this, you need to understand what these roles are and what they mean.

Trustees

The people who run your MySuper product or fund are called trustees, or directors. Super funds usually have between four and 16 trustees. Some funds that operate as "equal representation trustee boards" – e.g., in-house corporate super funds, government funds or industry funds – have half the trustees appointed by the fund sponsor (say, the employer) and half appointed by members or people representing the members (say, a union). More funds are now appointing independent trustees.

In many commercial products or funds, such as master trusts, the trustee role is played by an approved trustee company that is especially set up to provide these services. Approved trustees are registered with the industry regulator, the Australian Prudential Regulation Authority (APRA), and have to satisfy a range of licensing requirements before they can offer their services.

Trustees are not expected to be experts in all aspects of how to run a product or fund, but they are expected to know how to manage people who are. Your fund's trustees are there to represent you and make sure the fund is working properly for you and its other members. If anything goes wrong with the fund, the buck always stops with the trustees, and this motivates them to make sure things are working properly. A good trustee board will always listen to the members and will work to keep them informed about how the fund is performing.

Investment managers

Investment managers are expert companies that specialise in managing investments. They may also be called fund managers, money managers or asset managers.

Their job is to decide what assets to buy and when to sell or hold these investments to make the best return for the super fund members. Of course, while some investment managers are better than others, for the most part the crucial decision they have to make is the type of investments they buy into, such as shares, property or government bonds.

While the investment managers look after the investments, they do not operate the super fund itself. This means, for example, if you have problems with how your MySuper product or fund operates, what investments have been chosen or what other investment managers are being used, this is something you should complain to the trustees about.

MySuper products or super funds generally use up to 50 different investment managers, and of all the fees you pay two-thirds goes to these managers. Remember, it is the investment managers who run the investments, while the trustees run the actual super fund.

Asset consultants

When it comes to using investment managers, MySuper products and super funds have to choose from around 900 or more investment managers in Australia, and the thousands available overseas. Not surprisingly, they often need help from special advisers who are experts in understanding investment managers and how to choose between them. These experts are called asset consultants or sometimes investment consultants.

Asset consultants help super fund trustees decide how much money they should invest into particular types of investments or asset classes, e.g., how much money a fund should invest into overseas shares compared to Australian government bonds. Some personal master trusts that operate dozens, or even hundreds of different investment options, may also

Consumer warning: products not funds

Is your super with a product or an actual fund? Funds are run by trustees that are regulated by the government. A product is run by a finance company. Even though the product sits within a fund and the finance company itself is licensed, the product's investments are directed by the finance company, not the fund trustees.

As a result, the lines of control are a bit different.

If you choose to use a superannuation product run this way, you should check that you trust the finance company offering the product. This is because if something goes wrong it could be harder to sort out who is actually responsible. To address these concerns, some of these products now have advisory boards to act as informal trustees.

Administrators and platform providers

Superannuation trustees sometimes use specialist companies to help them administer their product or fund. These specialist administrators are experts in the government rules of operating a fund and making sure the fund meets all the compliance and regulatory requirements.

Administrators also make sure that every time an employer pays a contribution into an employee's super fund account this money is recorded properly. Annual reports, member statements and government compliance reports are all produced and managed by your super fund's administrators, and it is usually the fund's administrator that operates the call centre that answers when you email or ring up with an enquiry.

Administrators of master trusts are sometimes called 'platform providers', as they provide the back end investment platform that essentially makes up the master trust, in addition to just providing regular administration services. In doing this, platform providers offer a mix of asset consultancy expertise to the funds, and in this way they are usually more sophisticated in their operations than regular super fund administration companies.

:use investment research companies to help them choose and assess investment options before they are added to a super fund's investment menu.

In recent years, some super funds have started outsourcing their entire investment operations to asset consultants, who are then assigned the complete task of designing the investment strategy and choosing the investment managers for the super fund. This is called 'implemented consulting'.

This arrangement is generally used by only the biggest employers running in-house corporate super funds, as most usually outsource their whole fund — rather than just parts of the fund — to an industry fund or a master trust.

Some smaller industry funds have, however, started using implemented consultants so they can get access to the same economies of scale as bigger funds.

Because some asset consultants have been so successful with their advising services, they have now adapted these into their own master trusts that they offer to employers and consumers. When this happens, consultants cross the line from being just consultants to being fully fledged product operators, and this is how you must judge them.

Insurers

Insurers are the insurance companies used by your super fund to provide the life insurance policy that they offer you.

Custodians

Many MySuper products or super funds also use special companies called 'custodians' to hold their assets and to coordinate and keep track of the investment managers used by the super fund.

Custodians act as an important check for super funds because they help insulate the super fund from fraud and dubious investment transactions. If your fund has a custodian in place it means that if an investment fraud was perpetrated on the fund, the custodian would foot the bill, because a big part of their job is protecting the fund from fraud.

Most good MySuper products or super funds use only very large and highly expert custodians. If your fund, however, does not use a custodian that is separate to the super fund — that is, they try to handle this role themselves — make sure you understand how the super fund does this, because if it is not handled properly your super savings could be at risk.

Superannuation – the story so far

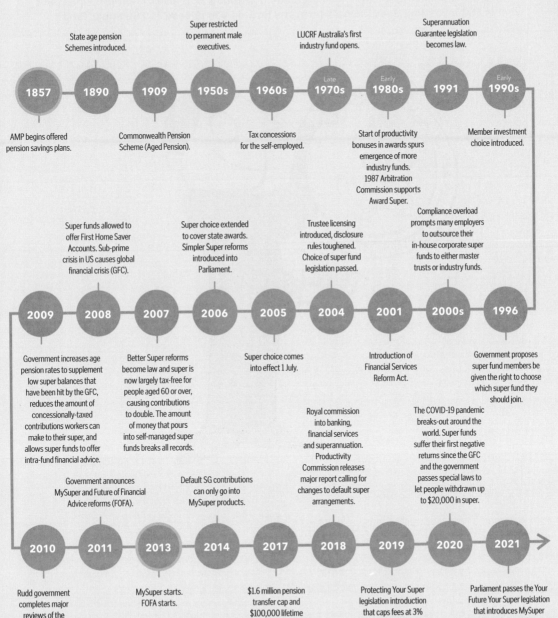

State age pension Schemes introduced.

Super restricted to permanent male executives.

LUCRF Australia's first industry fund opens.

Superannuation Guarantee legislation becomes law.

1857 **1890** **1909** **1950s** **1960s** Late **1970s** Early **1980s** **1991** Early **1990s**

AMP begins offered pension savings plans.

Commonwealth Pension Scheme (Aged Pension).

Tax concessions for the self-employed.

Start of productivity bonuses in awards spurs emergence of more industry funds. 1987 Arbitration Commission supports Award Super.

Member investment choice introduced.

Super funds allowed to offer First Home Saver Accounts. Sub-prime crisis in US causes global financial crisis (GFC).

Super choice extended to cover state awards. Simpler Super reforms introduced into Parliament.

Trustee licensing introduced, disclosure rules toughened. Choice of super fund legislation passed.

Compliance overload prompts many employers to outsource their in-house corporate super funds to either master trusts or industry funds.

2009 **2008** **2007** **2006** **2005** **2004** **2001** **2000s** **1996**

Government increases age pension rates to supplement low super balances that have been hit by the GFC, reduces the amount of concessionally-taxed contributions workers can make to their super, and allows super funds to offer intra-fund financial advice.

Better Super reforms become law and super is now largely tax-free for people aged 60 or over, causing contributions to double. The amount of money that pours into self-managed super funds breaks all records.

Super choice comes into effect 1 July.

Introduction of Financial Services Reform Act.

Government proposes super fund members be given the right to choose which super fund they should join.

Royal commission into banking, financial services and superannuation. Productivity Commission releases major report calling for changes to default super arrangements.

The COVID-19 pandemic breaks-out around the world. Super funds suffer their first negative returns since the GFC and the government passes special laws to let people withdrawn up to $20,000 in super.

Government announces MySuper and Future of Financial Advice reforms (FOFA).

Default SG contributions can only go into MySuper products.

2010 **2011** **2013** **2014** **2017** **2018** **2019** **2020** **2021**

Rudd government completes major reviews of the superannuation system and proposes increasing the SG rate to 12%.

MySuper starts. FOFA starts.

$1.6 million pension transfer cap and $100,000 lifetime non-concessional contribution cap introduced. Low-income tax offset scheme re-introduced.

Protecting Your Super legislation introduction that caps fees at 3% and stops super funds charging members for insurance they can't claim against.

Parliament passes the Your Future Your Super legislation that introduces MySuper stapling, the annual super fund performance test and toughens the obligations on trustees to act in the best interests of members.

Source: Rainmaker Information

ESG and super

More super fund members are choosing funds that follow ESG investment principles. But what is ESG investing, does it outperform and how do you choose an ESG super fund?

Millions of super fund members throughout Australia have become aware of the influence their fund's investments can have fighting climate change, minimising pollution, boosting the generation of renewable energy, reducing deforestation, discouraging the consumption of tobacco products, reducing inequality and discrimination and the sale of armaments, and fighting modern slavery.

When super fund members do this, they are choosing to invest according to a set of philosophies and principles that may be known variously as **ethical, responsible, sustainable, socially aware** or **impact investing**. An umbrella term that combines all these

elements is **ESG** investing, meaning to invest in such a way that promotes positive environmental, sustainability and governance (ESG) outcomes. At its simplest, ESG investing seeks to avoid investments that do harm, instead favouring investments that do good.

There are two main ways in which super fund members can choose an ESG super fund:
1. Choose an ESG super fund investment option that is explicitly labelled "ethical", "sustainable", "responsible" or "socially aware".
2. Choose a superannuation fund that, while it might not offer a specific ESG investment option, as a whole follows ESG investment principles.

How do ESG investments perform?

Choosing ESG superannuation funds might make members feel better, but how does it impact their account balances? To investigate this, Rainmaker Information analysed the investment returns of diversified balanced and growth super fund investment options and equities super fund investment options, over one, and three and five years, contrasting how ESG investment options performed compared to the overall market.

As shown in the chart, there is almost no difference, and where there is a difference in the sector averages it's ever so slight. These results mean that not only do ESG super fund investment options perform just as well as regular investments, they can sometimes do better.

But you should not invest into a super fund just because it is an ESG super fund. You should invest into it because it's proven itself to be a good superannuation fund. This is because if your superannuation fund is a good fund, it will run a good ESG investment option; if it's a weak fund, its ESG investments will probably also be weak.

ESG performance: overall vs ESG, 2021

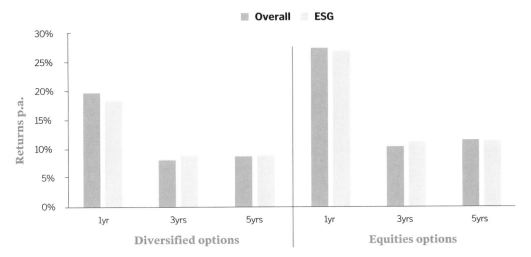

Source: Rainmaker Information

ESG super funds are active investors

When a super fund commits to follow ESG principles, and especially when it becomes a signatory to one of the various global ESG protocols, it is agreeing to become an active investor. This means it is agreeing to run its fund according to ESG principles, and seeks to positively influence the companies in which it invests by participating in shareholder meetings and taking active positions on company and public policy. Super fund trustee boards should not sign on these major ESG protocols if they are afraid of upsetting people, and members should expect their fund to sometimes be savagely criticised for what it does. Indeed, a super fund's own members may at times be its biggest critics.

To divest or not ... that is not the question.

Divestment is when a super fund sells down its investment in a particular company or industry to reduce its carbon impact or boost its social impact. For example, it may divest from a coal mining or armaments company. However, if an ESG super fund wishes to influence the corporate behaviour of that company, it needs to be a shareholder, otherwise why would the company listen to it?

This is why some ESG funds stay invested in companies that at first glance appear to not match their ESG values, even though they may be heavily criticised for doing so. Conversely, some ESG super funds have been accused of grandstanding when they announce a divestment because, while they may have reduced their carbon impact, they haven't actually reduced the economy's overall carbon impact. So it's a balancing act. There is no right, best, wrong or worst strategy. As a result, ESG super funds need to consider their own circumstances when making these decisions. But regardless of their decision, they must be prepared to explain it to their fund members.

Beware the pretenders

ESG investing has become very popular and there's a risk that some funds might try to talk-up their ESG credentials. To help you spot if your superannuation fund really is committed to ESG investment principles, Rainmaker Information has developed a framework that describes what to look for in an ESG super fund. This framework is described in the table on page 29.

In summary, all ESG superannuation funds should be able to demonstrate their commitments to high standards of governance and investment transparency, they should publish information and reports on their ESG activities and the impacts they are having, they should describe clearly their investment processes and, above all, they should have a strong investment track record.

Portfolio holdings disclosure

One of the most important ways to judge the credentials of a superannuation fund that claims to follow ESG investment principles is that it openly tells its fund members which investments it holds. This doesn't just mean it tells you it holds shares, properties and bonds, but which company shares, what properties and which bonds? Super funds that disclose this information are said to practise what is known as **portfolio holdings disclosure**.

While it's not compulsory for superannuation funds to practise portfolio holdings disclosure, it's one of best markers of a good ESG fund. It also helps you check what your superannuation fund isn't investing into. For example, if you don't want to be a member of superannuation fund that invests into

	Dimension	Description	Evidence points to look for. The fund:
A	Governance	The fund publicly declares its commitments to ESG principles.	1. Declares itself committed to ESG principles. 2. Publishes a statement of its values 3. Publishes information about its ESG credentials 4. Has a diverse leadership team 5. Is a signatory to at least one major ESG protocols group 6. Actively engages with stakeholders on ESG
B	Investment transparency	The fund discloses what it invests in and how it engages with companies into which it invests.	7. Practises Portfolio Holdings Disclosure 8. Publishes proxy voting reports
C	Publishes ESG reports	The fund reviews and discloses its environmental, climate change and social impacts.	9. Publishes environmental impact reports 10. Publishes carbon disclosure/impact reports 11. Publishes social impact reports
D	Investment processes	The fund discloses the investment practices though which it implements ESG.	12. Clearly explains how it makes its investment decisions 13. Publishes details of its investment screens 14. Publishes details of screen thresholds 15. Reports on the climate and social impacts of its investments
E	Performance	The fund's default option achieves at least above-average investment performance.	16. Achieves competitive investment returns 17. Demonstrates investment risk management 18. May offer ESG investment options

fossil fuel companies, there's no better way to check this than looking at your fund's portfolio holdings disclosure lists, which usually come in the form of its 50 largest Australian shareholdings, 50 largest international shareholdings, and 10 largest property and infrastructure investments.

How Australia's international treaties impact your super fund's ESG strategy

Australia's international ESG commitments can be split into two main groups: climate action commitments and social and governance commitments. Climate action commitments include following the Kyoto Protocol, the Doha Amendment, and the more recent Paris Agreement that involves the move to net-zero. Social and governance commitments include following Australia's commitment to the United Nations Sustainable Development Goals (SDG) and Australia's own Modern Slavery Act.

Superannuation funds and investment managers that claim to practise ESG have integrated many of the principles contained in these treaties, agreements and protocols into their investment philosophies.

The Paris Agreement and net-zero

Australia's climate action commitments centre on the **Paris Agreement**, which came into force in November 2016. It is a legally binding international treaty on climate change action signed by 196

KEY POINTS

- ESG investing is a philosophical investment framework that promotes positive environmental, sustainability and governance outcomes in the economy and among the super fund's stakeholders.

- Super funds that practise ESG principles are very open about how they operate, make their investment decisions and what they invest in.

- Super funds that invest this way are just as likely to earn the same returns as funds that don't.

nations. The goal of the Paris Agreement is to limit global warming to below two degrees compared to pre-industrial levels, though the agreement states that 1.5 degrees is the preferred aspirational target.

The Paris Agreement is based on international commitments nations made as part of the United Nations Framework Convention on Climate Change (UNFCCC) and the Kyoto Protocol, which was itself based on the 1992 UN Climate Change Convention.

The core way that nations are expected to help reduce climate change is by reducing their greenhouse gas (GHG) emissions. The major plank of this is the push for as many nations as possible to adopt Net Zero by 2050, which means that by this time nations will be expected to be producing zero GHG emissions, or rather net-zero after taking account of any abatement, crediting or offsetting arrangements.

Other measures that make up the Paris Treaty are that developed nations will provide financial assistance to developing nations to reduce their own GHG emissions, that all nations will try to develop technology solutions to support climate action and developed nations will support developing nations build their capacity to reduce GHG emissions.

It is up to each nation to decide how will it achieve its own climate action target. However, under the Paris Agreement, they must publicly commit to emissions reduction targets known as **Nationally Determined Contributions** (NDCs). These plans must be lodged with the UNFCCC that administers the global agreement. Before the November 2021 COP26 Climate Change Conference in Glasgow, only about half the nations that signed the Paris Agreement had submitted NDCs. But more did this at the conference.

This heavy focus on the Paris Agreement and net-zero is why so many superannuation funds are incorporating their own net-zero commitments into their investment strategies. They implement these by either investing in companies that themselves have made net-zero commitments, they divest away from companies that don't support net-zero, or they have made a commitment to try to encourage companies in which they are investing to commit to net-zero.

Sustainable Development Goals

The Sustainable Development Goals (SDG) are a set of social and cultural goals and targets set up through the United Nations. The list of globally

United Nations Principles for Responsible Investment

Superannuation funds and investment managers around the world committed to ESG and responsible investing worked with the United Nations to in 2008 launch an investment framework based on the principles contained in these treaties, agreements and protocols. This framework is known as the Principles for Responsible Investment. Two-thirds of Australia's superannuation system is overseen by super funds that follow this framework.

agreed SDGs and their implementation framework was formally adopted in 2015 by a vote of the General Assembly.

There are 17 core SDGs, which the United Nations says "are an urgent call for action by all countries – developed and developing – in a global partnership. They recognise that ending poverty and other deprivations must go hand-in-hand with strategies that improve health and education, reduce inequality, and spur economic growth – all while tackling climate change and working to preserve our oceans and forests."

The SDGs were first officially recognised at the 1992 Rio de Janeiro, Brazil, Earth Summit, where more than 178 countries adopted **Agenda 21**, which was a comprehensive plan of action to implement the SDGs. The Earth Summit was followed up by the Millennium Declaration signed in 2000 at the UN headquarters in New York.

This declaration included the establishment of eight Millennium Development Goals (MDGs) that aimed to reduce extreme poverty by 2015.

Several superannuation funds have actively incorporated the SDGs into their investment strategies. Some have even designed investment options that aim to invest into companies and bonds that explicitly support the SDGs.

The Modern Slavery Act

As part of Australia's commitment to support the United Nations Guiding Principles on Business and Human Rights, the Modern Slavery Act was passed by the Australian Parliament in 2019. The Act requires all large businesses operating in Australia, including superannuation funds, with annual revenue of $100 million or more, to lodge a Modern Slavery Statement with the Australian Border Force.

Practices that constitute modern slavery can include human trafficking, slavery, servitude, forced labour, debt bondage, forced marriage, and the worst forms of child labour. About 50 super funds have so far published a Modern Slavery Statement, and if your super fund is one of them, reviewing it provides a great insight into its philosophy and investment strategy.

The 17 sustainable development goals

1.	No poverty	10.	Reduced inequalities
2.	Zero hunger	11.	Sustainable cities and communities
3.	Good health and wellbeing	12.	Responsible consumption
4.	Quality education	13.	Climate action
5.	Gender equality	14.	Life below water
6.	Clean water and sanitation	15.	Life on land
7.	Affordable and clean energy	16.	Peace, justice and strong institutions
8.	Decent work and economic growth	17.	Partnerships for the goals
9.	Industry, innovation and infrastructure		

COVID-19 catch-up superannuation contributions

If you were one of the 3.5 million people who made an emergency COVID-19 withdrawal from your superannuation account, if you can afford to, you should consider re-contributing that money.

The full effects of the COVID-19 physical and mental health, financial and economic crisis are now being realised. But one of the hidden aspects of the crisis, with huge long-run implications, is how it has damaged the superannuation savings of the millions of super fund members who needed to make an emergency withdrawal from their superannuation.

Under a government policy measure known as the **COVID-19 Early Release Scheme**, fund members could withdraw up to $20,000 in two parts over two financial years. The scheme is no longer open but the superannuation regulator, the Australian Prudential Regulation Authority, said 3.5 million fund members withdrew a collective total of $36 billion.

Forty percent of these applications were from people who made two withdrawals, showing how desperate they were to access the money in their superannuation account.

Worse still, figures released by the Australian Taxation Office revealed that while people under age 35 make up just one-third of all superannuation fund members, they made up more than half of all the people who applied for an emergency COVID-19 superannuation withdrawal. Many of these people withdrew almost all their superannuation savings, taking them back to having no superannuation.

Given that 2020/21 was the best year for superannuation returns in 34 years, these fund members have been doubly penalised.

The COVID-19 re-contribution scheme

Recognising that many of the people who made these emergency superannuation withdrawals may now want to catch up to their pre-withdrawal balance, the government introduced a special **re-contribution of COVID-19 early release amounts into superannuation measure** to help them rebuild their balance.

Under this provision, fund members can put the same amount of money they withdrew from their superannuation fund under the COVID-19 Early Release Scheme back into their superannuation account and it won't count towards their **non-concessional contribution cap**.

It's, of course, highly unlikely that anyone who made an emergency COVID-19 superannuation withdrawal will now be contributing anywhere near their $110,000 annual non-concessional contribution cap.

Instead, people in that position may be better off re-contributing that money back into their superannuation account as a personal voluntary contribution so they can claim it as a tax deduction.

KEY POINTS

- When the COVID-19 financial crisis was in full swing, the government introduced special laws to enable you to withdraw up to $20,000 from your superannuation account.

- Most of the people who took up this offer were young and many of them cleaned out their superannuation account.

- If you can afford to, you should consider re-contributing that money back into your superannuation account.

Worth knowing: your superannuation contribution limits

- Anyone of working age can contribute up to $27,500 in **concessional contributions** into their superannuation account from their pre-tax salary, meaning it will be taxed at 15% rather than at their probably much higher marginal taxation rate. Money your employer contributes to superannuation for you under the 10% SG rules is included in this $27,500 cap.

- Provided you stay within this concessional contribution limit of $27,500, you can also make additional contributions either as **salary sacrifice** or as **personal contributions**. In salary sacrifice contributions, your employer pays some of your wages into your superannuation pre-tax, meaning they are taxed at 15% rather than at your marginal tax rate. Personal contributions are made from your after-tax income. You can usually claim a tax deduction for personal contributions.

- Most people are eligible to contribute another $110,000 into their superannuation account as **non-concessional contributions**, but it will not attract a tax concession, meaning it will be paid from after-tax income.

Should I see a financial adviser?

Financial advisers are professional experts who can help you choose a super fund, understand your investment profile and tailor your insurance protection.

KEY POINTS

- Financial advisers are professional experts who will design a financial plan for you.

- They are experts in investments, super, insurance and managing your taxation.

- Read your financial adviser's financial services guide, which is like a product disclosure statement for financial advisers.

Financial planning is a range of professional services that spans helping you understand your superannuation savings and investment goals and showing you how you can build and protect your wealth. It can also help you set up the right financial structures and show you how to develop good financial habits to position you for the future.

Almost all super funds offer financial planning, which they deliver either in person using people known as financial advisers, or in print, online or over the phone.

For people who need superannuation advice, they can help you by providing independent counsel on how much you should contribute to superannuation, how you should structure your contributions so you get the most taxation advantages, what investment choices you should make, whether you should use a low-cost fund or a platform, or when it is appropriate to set up a self-managed super fund (SMSF).

Robo-investing

Robo-investing, sometimes called robo-advice, is streamlined automated financial advice delivered online through a website or smart device app. Robo-investing usually covers how to identify your investment profile and design for you a simple asset allocation strategy. It may also cover allocating you into exchange traded products with which the company that runs the robo-investing website has an association.

Financial advice and super funds

In this guide we have described how you can navigate all the factors to consider when choosing super funds, and questions you need to ask. We have also explained how you can access super funds, how you should compare them, and how to monitor your investment performance, insurance and fees.

While this information has been tailored for people who are comfortable doing their own research and making their own decisions and investment choices, not everyone is ready to do this by themselves. This is why many fund members, including those who are highly experienced, will have a relationship with a financial adviser, even if it is just to get a second opinion.

Choosing the right financial adviser

When choosing a financial adviser, make sure you find one who has all the necessary skills and qualifications, and who is part of a reputable advisory organisation committed to serving their clients' long-term needs.

When considering which financial adviser to consult with, you should check they are a member of a relevant professional association bound by a code of ethics and rules of professional conduct. Are they registered with the ASIC Financial Advice Register? Do they have an Australian Financial Services Licence (AFSL)? Are they an authorised representative of an AFS Licensee? If they aren't, walk away.

!

Consumer warning: Be wary of financial advisers who won't show you their FSG until after you've met with them.

SelectAdviser

To find a financial adviser near you, visit selectadviser.com.au. This website is run by Rainmaker Information, the publisher of *The Good Super Guide*. It will help you find financial advisers in your area and it will display the adviser's professional profile, including their expertise and qualifications.

Financial services guide (FSG)

A financial services guide is a like a product disclosure statement for financial advisers. It describes who an adviser represents, how they get paid, the services they provide and which companies they are associated with. Good advisers will have their FSG on full display on the website.

ETPs, robo-investing and managed accounts

Exchange traded products (ETPs), robo-investing and managed accounts are gaining popularity among superannuation fund members. What are they, how do they work and what do they cost?

KEY POINTS

- ETPs and robo-investment services can give you access to investment options at much lower fees than what is being charged by regular superannuation funds.

- But if you want to use these for your superannuation, you will need to put them inside your self-managed fund or use a superannuation managed account.

- If you don't, your investment returns will be taxed at your full marginal tax rate, not at the concessional 15% superannuation rate.

There are now more ways to invest your superannuation than ever before. As you begin exploring some of these newer types of choices or solutions, you will probably come across terms like exchange traded products, robo-investing and managed accounts. But what are they and how can you use them for your superannuation?

ETPs

An ETP is a type of managed fund or superannuation fund investment option that is tradable on a stock exchange. Exchange traded products may also be called exchange traded funds.

ETPs are becoming so popular because they combine some of the best benefits of owning company shares and managed funds by allowing you to access a portfolio of securities and trade units in that ETP on the stock exchange easily and cheaply.

But being tradable on the stock exchange does not mean it's listed on the stock exchange. By this we mean that you are simply using the stock exchange's trading platforms to buy and sell units in the ETP. While the price of a regular listed company share is determined by the demand for it, the price of units in an ETP is determined by the underlying value of those units.

Most ETPs are purpose-built to replicate a particular index such as the S&P/ASX 200 or the S&P 500 which covers the US stockmarket. But some track niche indexes only followed by that particular ETP, while some are regular actively managed funds that just happen to be accessible through the stock exchange.

ETP portfolios may include Australian shares, international shares, fixed-income securities, listed property trusts, commodities like gold and precious metals, currencies, or a combination of those asset classes.

The structure of ETPs means they can often operate at much lower fees than regular investments. For example, ETPs charge on average one-third the regular investment fee of other investment funds, and ETPs that invest into plain vanilla indexes like the S&P/ASX 200 might charge fees as low as 0.10% p.a.

There is no entry cost when you invest into an ETP or exit costs when you sell your units. But you may have to pay broking charges and the costs of changing investment allocations in the fund.

Robo-investing

Robo-investing, sometimes called robo-advice, is an online financial planning and investment service that offers you recommendations, usually based on a computer algorithm.

The way it works is that when you engage a robo-investment provider, they will usually ask you some questions designed to figure out your risk profile and which types of investments interest you. This information is assessed by the algorithm and, based on this, it will recommend an investment package.

This investment package will usually be an investment fund that has been specifically designed for people with a risk profile like yours. It is usually assembled using a suite of low-cost managed funds such as ETPs. Because robo-investment services are providing you with an investment with a certain amount of "tailoring", they will charge a small fee on top of the investment fees already built into the ETPs they use to assemble your investment package..

Rainmaker Information found that in 2021 these fees can average just 0.4% p.a., including an average 0.3% p.a. for the advice and recommendation service and access to their support and smart device apps that you can use to monitor and manage your investments. Some robo-investing services also have a premium higher-fee service that allows clients to access human financial advisers.

Managed accounts

Managed accounts are the latest generation of investment administration platforms that generally have very sophisticated investment menus and more advanced taxation management features. They are built on the latest web-based cloud computing technology that lets you monitor and manage your investments using your computer or smart device, often in real-time.

Managed accounts generally cost a little bit less than regular superannuation funds, noting that they usually charge an administration fee of about 0.5% p.a. plus the investment fee that goes to the specific investment choices you have chosen.

Some managed accounts are now structured as a superannuation fund, so you can choose them as your superannuation provider. This means the managed account is connected to a regulated superannuation fund that pays tax on your behalf.

ETPs can cost much less than regular super fund investment options

Research by Rainmaker Information in 2021 revealed that while the typical investment fee for an Australian shares superannuation fund investment option is 0.8% p.a., the average investment fee for an Australian shares ETP that tracks the S&P/ASX 200 can be as low as 0.1% p.a. It only makes sense to pay the higher fees if your superannuation fund regularly beats its market index. If it doesn't, investing in the ETP may be worth considering. The good news is that many superannuation funds offer ETPs in their investment menus or in their **Member Direct option**.

How to package ETPs, robo-investing and managed accounts into your superannuation

ETPs, robo-investing and most managed accounts are just investments, meaning they are not superannuation funds. If you want to use these investments for your superannuation, you will need to place these investments into a self-managed super fund or superannuation managed account.

If you don't, your investment returns will be taxed at your regular marginal tax rate, which could be as high as 47%, rather than at the concessional 15% superannuation rate.

Investment menus explained

The backbone of a super fund is its investment menu. What is it, how does it work, and how do you navigate your way through it?

KEY POINTS

- A superannuation fund's investment menu is the list of investment choices it offers.

- Choices can include choice of investment strategy, choice of investment manager and even lifecycle choices.

- If you can't decide, your super fund might assign you into its default MySuper investment option, or suggest you put your money into a balanced option or one matching your age.

A super fund's investment menu is the full list of all the fund's investment options or choices. When trying to make sense of these investment choices, or just the investment strategy underpinning your MySuper product, there are three main things for you to think about:

- the investment strategy
- who will manage your money
- how many investment options you need.

Your investment strategy – diversified or specialist?

Your investment strategy describes the type and mix of assets you want your investments to include. Do you want to spread your investments across lots of different classes of assets like shares, property, bonds and cash; or do you want to invest only into specific asset classes?

If you want to spread your money across several asset classes, this is called a **diversified** investment strategy. If you want to focus upon a single asset class, this is called a **specialist** investment strategy. Diversified options can also be called **multisector** or even **multi-asset** options, while specialist asset class options can also be called just sector options.

Growth, balanced or conservative?

Diversified investment options are categorised according to the proportion of growth assets they have. There are four main types:

- Growth – more than 75% in growth assets.
- Balanced – 55% to 75% in growth assets.
- Moderate – 35% to 55% in growth assets. These may also be called capital stable options.
- Conservative – less than 35% in growth assets. These may also be called capital guaranteed options.

The major advantage of using diversified investment options is that the super fund makes the decisions about the mix of assets to buy for you. But as you become more experienced as a super fund member, you may want to make these decisions yourself, whether that means you choose just one asset class specialist option or you mix your own selection; this is why many funds now offer lots of specialist asset class investment options.

The irony is that by mixing several specialist investment options together, you may be effectively constructing your own diversified investment portfolio anyway, albeit one that is more customised.

Growth, income or defensive?

Investment strategies are usually categorised by how much money is placed in growth assets and how much is in income assets. Growth assets such as shares or property are so named because they are meant to grow in value over time, and income assets such as bonds and cash are so named because they are intended to hold their value and deliver regular income.

Income assets are also known as defensive assets as they are much less likely to fall in value; meanwhile, bonds are also known as fixed interest. The subtlety is that some growth assets can also be defensive and deliver income – e.g., shares can deliver dividend income and property can deliver rental income – while some income assets like infrastructure can also rise in value. It's not always as straightforward as the textbooks tell us.

The normal rule of thumb is that the more growth assets in your investment portfolio, the better your chances of making more money over the long term. But your returns may jump around more from year to year, i.e., their returns are more volatile and so they have what is known as higher investment risk. Conversely, the more income or defensive assets in your investment portfolio, the lower the expected

longer-term returns, but that should come with lower volatility and less investment risk.

This is what experts mean when they talk about the **risk-return trade-off**.

Lifecycle investment choices

A new style of investment option that is becoming more popular in Australia following its wide use in the US and the introduction of MySuper is what are known as lifecycle, lifestage or age-based options. These are diversified investment options where your super fund assigns you into an investment strategy depending on how old you are or, its flipside, when you expect to retire. These options are described in more detail on page 20.

For example, if you are under the age of 45, meaning you were born in the 1970s or later (i.e., you are gen X), your super fund might assign you into an option it could variously call a 1970s or 20-year strategy. Because you are likely to be in that investment option for about another two decades, the investment strategy is very growth asset oriented with a high exposure to shares and property.

What if you can't decide?

Having many investment options is great if you are comfortable making investment decisions, but not everyone is ready or able to make these decisions. If you are one of the many millions of super fund members in Australia who can't decide which investment option to choose, then your super fund will assign you either into its default investment option, which is usually a balanced or growth option, or a lifecycle option, or it will suggest you choose its main balanced option. In workplace funds these default options are called **MySuper** products.

If you are a baby boomer aged 60 who was born in 1960 and expects to retire in about five to 10 years, your super fund might similarly assign you into an investment option with lower exposure to growth assets but higher exposure to income or defensive assets.

Another important thing for you to consider about these types of investment options is how does your fund transition your account balance into different investment strategies as you get older? The two main approaches are to either physically swap you from one option to another – and thus implicitly force you to sell units in one option and buy units in another, triggering higher embedded tax costs – or adjust the investment strategy across the investment option's whole portfolio based on the average age of all the people in that option.

Who manages your money?

Do you want to use just one investment manager, or do you want your money spread across several investment managers? In the same way that diversifying across several asset classes helps you control investment risk, you can also reduce investment risk by spreading your money across several investment managers.

Investment options that do this are called **multi-manager** options. In contrast, **single-manager** options are those that give all your money to just one investment manager. But if you use a diversified investment option to spread your investments across lots of asset classes and you do this through a multi-manager investment that uses too many investment managers, you could end up with so much diversification across asset classes and investment managers that you will effectively just be matching the market.

How many investment options?

The next question is how many investment options do you want to be able to choose from? Do you want only a limited number of choices, a medium number of choices or lots of choices? This question is important because the more choices and flexibility you want, the higher your super fund's fees will probably be.

It's also worth noting that if you choose super funds with more investment options, you may need to work closely with your financial adviser because the more choices you have usually means the more help and advice you will need to take full advantage of all the options available.

The twist is that funds with low fees usually have fewer investment options, while funds with high numbers of investment options usually have higher fees. This is why, when you are choosing superannuation funds and choosing between investment menus, you are also implicitly choosing the type of fund you want to join and what fees you expect to pay.

The following table illustrates how this works.

Your investment menu

Number of options	Primary segments	Choice of investment strategy	Choice of investment manager	Overall fees
1	MySuper products	No	No	Low
2-15	Mainly industry funds	Yes	No	Low-medium
16-80	Mainly retail funds	Yes	Limited	Medium-high
More than 80	Retail funds only	Yes	Extensive	Medium-high

Source: Rainmaker Information

Investment performance explained

Making sense of your MySuper product or fund's investment performance figures can be difficult. This easy guide will explain how they work and what they really mean.

When a MySuper product or super fund talks about investment performance, they can use many terms that confuse members. They even confuse many people who run super funds. So, what does investment performance actually mean?

Investment performance describes how much your super product or fund is earning for you each year, each month, each day. Think of it as the investment profit they are making for you. Investment performance is also sometimes called the **investment return**, **performance** or sometimes just the **return**.

Another problem is that some products or funds report investment performance before they have deducted tax, some may deduct the tax and the investment fees but not the ongoing percentage-based fees, and some may deduct all taxes and all the percentage-based fees. Almost none, however, will deduct the dollar-based flat fees when declaring their investment performance even though for people starting out in super, who only have a small amount of superannuation savings, this fee is their biggest headache.

Earnings rates and crediting rates

If you are a member of an in-house corporate, public sector or industry fund (known as a not-for-profit super fund), your MySuper product or super fund will often talk about its investment performance in terms of its earnings rate and its crediting rate.

The earnings rate is the investment performance earned by the super fund after paying the investment managers their fees but before paying the

KEY POINTS

- Investment returns can be described differently by different types of funds.

- The investment return money deposited into your account after all fees and charges have been deducted is what you should really worry about..

investment taxes and other ongoing fees. Think of this number as what it earns from the capital markets before deducting its own operating costs. This earnings figure can also be thought of as how good your super fund's trustees are at picking investment managers.

The crediting rate, on the other hand, is the investment return after all taxes and all the percentage-based management fees have been deducted, where these management fees include ongoing administration and investment fees. *Money* magazine goes one extra step when publishing its crediting rate performance tables. We make an allowance for the impact of dollar-based member fees.

For the average superannuation investor, the relationship between a product's or fund's earnings rate and its crediting rate is also very important to understand because it can tell you much about how a super fund operates. This is because from their earnings rate they pay investment taxes and other costs associated with operating the super fund. The bigger the difference, the more fees and costs are being deducted. For example, if your product or fund earned 10% but only credited 8% into your account, it means your true level of fees is the difference, that being 2%.

Reserving accounts

Some super funds may also divert some of their earnings rate into a reserving account to help build up a nest egg so they can top up returns in bad years. The downside is that in good years the returns will not be as good as they should be because some of the return has been diverted into this reserving account. Some people think these reserving accounts are bad because they take returns away from members in good years. Others think they are good because they boost members' returns in bad years. The truth is they are neither bad nor good, but if your fund uses one it is important to understand how it works and why they have it.

The only twist with reserving is that it can penalise people who don't stay with the fund for a long time as some of the fund's earnings are hived off for that rainy day that may not come around until after you have left the fund. The flipside is that if you join in a bad performance year you could get a better return than funds that don't use reserving. It's a case of swings and roundabouts.

Fees affect performance

While in-house corporate, government and industry super funds speak in terms of earnings and crediting rates, retail super funds, being corporate and

---

How superannuation performance is published

When *Money* magazine publishes performance figures it is assumed that fund members pay the maximum fees because this allows us to convert the performance figures into crediting rate equivalents.

Doing it this way is consistent with the Australian Securities and Investments Commission's (ASIC) guidelines, and it means the performance figures we publish will be the least you should expect. If you have a fee deal from your MySuper product or fund and you receive a fee discount you will get even more money in your account.

To make sure we are comparing performance figures properly we always check if the investment return being publicly declared is before or after taking tiered management and investment fees into account.

If fees haven't been fully deducted we will apply these fees to make sure the investment return we publish is as close to the actual crediting rate as possible. We do this because some master trusts may say their performance is after fees, but they really mean that only the investment fees have been deducted.

The table on page 43 shows you how this works.

personal master trusts, usually just speak in terms of performance. This can mean, depending upon the fund, either the earnings or the crediting rate, or something in between. But it's not as confusing as it seems because in many cases they effectively mean crediting rates anyway, which you will recall are just the returns after all percentage-based fees have been deducted. The sting in the tail, however, is that many master trusts have a tiered fee structure.

A tiered fee structure is when the fees differ depending how much you have invested with the fund or how much is in an employer's combined company account. For example, if you have less than $50,000 in your super fund account, you may pay 1.4% in fees, but if you have more than $200,000 in your account, you may pay fees of only 0.7%.

This means that two people in the same super fund may be paying quite different levels of fees and as a result receive different crediting rates; remember that the crediting rate is effectively the earnings rate less all the fees. These differing fees in the one fund can also mean that while low-balance members may be better off in an industry fund, members with higher balances who qualify for fee discounts may sometimes be better off in a retail fund, i.e., a master trust.

Flat dollar fees

If your MySuper product or fund charges a flat dollar fee, such as a member fee or a policy fee, it is usually paid after your crediting rate or after-fee performance has been declared and paid into your account. These member fees can have a significant impact upon your true return. For example, if you have $10,000 in super, even if your member fee is just $1 per week, it effectively means that an extra 0.5% will be deducted from your account.

Of course, as your super account grows, the impact of this member fee diminishes. For example, if you have $100,000 in superannuation, the impact of this member fee is only 0.05%. The lesson here is that flat dollar fees can impact people with low super account balances more than they realise. Most retail superannuation funds do not charge flat dollar member fees, but most industry funds do. The thing to watch, though, is that funds with member fees should have low percentage-based fees.

KEY POINTS

- Some funds have 'reserves' to smooth the investment return 'roller coaster'.

- When comparing super funds, make sure you compare similar types of funds.

Deconstruct your super fund's investment returns

	Not-for-profit fund	Corporate master trust	Personal master trust
Capital gains from markets	10.0%	10.0%	10.0%
Less investment fees + taxes	0.7%	0.7%	0.7%
Fund earnings rates	**9.3%**	**9.3%**	**9.3%**
Less reserving	0.6%	–	–
Less other fees	0.2%	1.0%	1.4%
Your crediting rate	**8.5%**	**8.3%**	**7.9%**

Source: Rainmaker Information

Super fund performance news 2021

Superannuation fund investment performance bounced back strongly in 2020/21 after the turmoil of COVID-19, making that financial year one of the best yet for super fund returns.

The Rainmaker MySuper investment performance index ended the 2020/21 financial year with an annual average return of 18.8%, its highest in 34 years. This was a massive turnaround from the previous year when the Rainmaker MySuper Index returned just -0.9%.

Not only was this a great recovery story, but it is only the third time the annual financial year return was above 15% in the last three and half decades. This was an impressive outcome considering investment markets in and outside Australia have still not shaken free of COVID-19.

The story gets even better over the medium and long term. MySuper index returns over three years were 8.0% p.a., over five years 8.6% p.a. and over 10 years 8.3% p.a. The ultra long-run story was just as impressive: 6.2% p.a. over 20 years and 7.2% p.a. over 30 years. This means the average MySuper default superannuation investment option is delivering almost five percentage points per annum above the long-term inflation rate, significantly beating even their most optimistic investment objectives.

While these figures reflect average returns across industry, choosing a high-performing superannuation product is still the key to securing your retirement nest egg. Demonstrating this difference between an average fund and the highest-performing fund, while members in an average fund have more than doubled their account balance in the last decade, members of the top funds would have seen their balances triple.

Asset class returns

Super funds invest across a mix of asset classes primarily categorised as growth or conservative, depending on whether they hold lots of equities and property or are tilted towards fixed-interest bonds and cash. The returns they achieve as a rule generally reflect the combined returns of these asset classes and how each fund mixes them together. The spectacular 2020/21 returns for MySuper, diversified and asset class specific sector products were mainly driven by high returns in three asset classes: Australian equities, international equities and property.

Performance test

In 2021 the government introduced a superannuation fund performance test. The government designed the test, which is administered by the superannuation regulator, the Australian Prudential Regulation Authority. The test currently applies only to MySuper products and measures the extent to which the product beat its asset class benchmarks over the past seven years. In 2022 the test will be extended to measure this value-add over eight years.

In September 2021, MySuper products were told whether they passed or failed. The 13 products that failed have already told their members. If they fail again in 2022, they will not be allowed to accept new members.

Superannuation investment options invested into Australian equities earned an average 26.9% in the financial year,28.0% for international equities and 21.3% for property. The other asset classes in the mix were Australian bonds, international bonds and cash, all earning returns of less than 1.0%, with Australian bonds actually going backwards.

Comparing the average return in each sector or asset class with their market peer index return adds a new angle to the story. It shows that as high as some of the returns were, superannuation funds still on average only matched the market or outperformed in international equities, property, international bonds and cash but underperformed in Australian equities and Australian bonds. This reminds us that even in a record-breaking year, super funds' investment performance may not always be as high as it could be.

It is worth noting, however, that this is an improvement over the 2019/20 financial year, when the asset class performance gaps between the superannuation asset class averages and their index returns were much higher than they were this financial year.

Returns in each asset sector, to 30 June, 2021
(Percent returns after all fees, pa)

	1 yr	5 yrs	10 yrs
Diversified			
MySuper/Default option	18.8%	8.6%	8.3%
Growth	22.6%	9.6%	9.2%
Balanced	16.6%	7.8%	7.8%
Capital stable	9.0%	5.0%	5.4%
Specialist			
Australian shares	26.9%	10.4%	8.6%
International shares	28.0%	12.6%	11.2%
Property	21.3%	5.5%	8.2%
Australian fixed interest	-0.4%	2.1%	3.5%
International fixed interest	0.5%	2.3%	3.7%
Cash	0.0%	1.0%	1.8%

Long-term super returns, to 30 June, 2021
(Percent returns after all fees, pa)

Years	1	5	10	15	20	25	30
Per year	18.8%	8.6%	8.3%	6.1%	6.2%	7.0%	7.2%

KEY POINTS

- Default MySuper products have just delivered an average 18.8%, their best performance in 34 years.

- Driving the result were stunningly high returns from equities and property.

- The best superannuation funds achieved investment outcomes double those achieved by the lowest performers.

These asset class investment outcomes mean that growth products with high exposure to equities and property achieved an average 22.6% return in 2020/21 compared to the 16.6% achieved by the average balanced product. Conversely, capital stable products that hold a larger proportion of their assets in conservative investments, like fixed interest bonds and cash, achieved average returns of 9.0%.

The same pattern held up over 10 years. Growth products averaged 9.2% p.a., balanced products 7.8% p.a. and capital stable products 5.4% p.a. MySuper products, as expected, delivered 10-year returns of 8.3% p.a., which sat right between these growth and balanced sector averages.

Yet again, results like these show us why it is important to diversify your investments and focus on the medium to longer term, which is why most people hold their superannuation in a MySuper product or in a growth or balanced investment choice.

Best versus the worst

While these impressive average superannuation returns are a reasonable benchmark of what members should be expecting from their fund, it is extremely important that you do not tolerate low-ranking returns, especially if they are sustained. For example, in 2020/21, while the average MySuper product achieved 18.8%, the best achieved 26.5% and the worst achieved 12.8%. This is a range from best to worst of 13.7 percentage points.

This gap comes about because each year the best-performing superannuation fund usually achieves two to three times the return of the lowest-performing superannuation fund. Viewed another way, during the past decade the average annual performance gap between the best and worst MySuper products was a staggering 10 percentage points. This is many times greater than the range

Long-term super fund returns – Default/MySuper

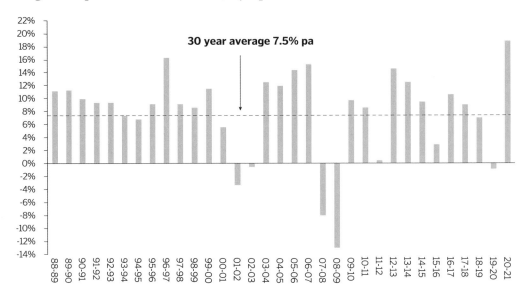

Source: Rainmaker Information

in fees between the cheapest and most expensive funds demonstrating why remaining a member of a low-performing, ie. low-ranking, fund is much more damaging to your savings than being in a fund charging excessive fees.

Showing how this works in practice, if you were in the top-performing super fund each year for the past decade, you would have averaged 9.6% p.a. But if you were in the lowest-performing fund every year, your 10-year return would be just 4.8% p.a., exactly half.

Lifecycle investment returns

Lifecycle MySuper products are those where the investment strategy is determined by the age of the fund member. As members of these products get older, they are moved into sub-options designed for their age group, i.e., as you get older, the more conservative your asset mix becomes.

The idea behind lifecycle investing is that when members are young they have many decades until they are expected to retire and should be investing more of their superannuation in high-performing, albeit higher-risk, assets like equities and property. But as they get older and approach retirement, their tolerance for investment risk reduces, so their exposure to equities and property is wound back in favour of more conservative asset classes like fixed interest and cash.

This year, unlike last year, was very good for lifecycle investment products. Lifecycle investment options for young members with heavy emphasis on equities were able to reap big benefits from the stockmarkets' high returns, earning substantially higher returns than the members in regular diversified single-strategy MySuper products that invest the same way regardless how old are the members of the fund. While single-strategy MySuper products earned an average 17.4%, lifecycle products for people aged under 50 years earned an average 21.8%.

For members aged 50 and above, the average MySuper lifecycle option returned 14.3% mainly due to a shift of asset allocation from growth to conservative, the reason being they become more focused on preserving capital. But it is at this stage of many fund members' lives when the power of compounding comes into play. Though every positive return adds multi-fold to members' account balances, on the flipside it hits harder when the returns are lower than they might expect.

These lifecycle investment return results mean that even if you choose a lifecycle investment strategy for your superannuation, it is still crucial that you compare its investment returns at least once a year. You should not take a set-and-forget approach.

MySuper lifecycle investment returns, to 30 June, 2021

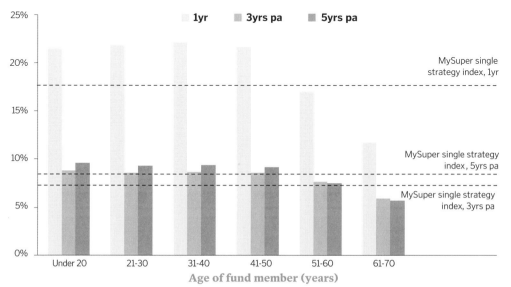

Source: Rainmaker Information

MySuper investment performance

The table below describes investment returns after fees and taxes that fund members would have received from each MySuper product.

MySuper product name	Annual average investment returns, net of all fees, 30 June, 2021				
	1 year	3 years	5 years	7 years	10 years
Active Super Accumulation Scheme	23.5	9.5	10.6	9.4	9.2
AMG Corporate Super	17.9	7.7	7.3		
AMIST Super Employer	16.0	6.8			
ANZ Staff Super - Employee	17.1	7.7	8.7		8.4
ANZ Smart Choice Super - Employer	22.2	8.7	9.3	8.3	
Australian Catholic - Employer	20.7	8.1			
ADF Super	17.9	7.8	8.4		
Australian Ethical Super	17.5	9.8	9.1	8.3	8.0
AustralianSuper	20.2	9.3	10.2	9.4	9.5
AvSuper Corporate	20.5	7.8	8.6	7.7	8.3
Aware Super - Employer Sponsored	17.8	8.6	9.5	8.3	8.7
Bendigo SmartStart - Employer	21.9	9.1	9.1	8.4	
BT Super	25.4	9.0	9.5		8.5
BUSSQ MySuper	17.0	7.8	8.3	8.2	8.6
CareSuper	17.1	7.6	8.8	8.3	8.8
Catholic Super	16.4	6.9	8.3	8.0	8.1
Cbus Industry Super	19.1	8.6	9.6	9.0	9.3
Christian Super	17.0	7.5	7.6	6.9	7.5
Club Plus Industry Division	15.5	6.6	8.4	7.6	7.7
CFS - FirstChoice Employer Super	25.7	7.9	9.1	7.7	
CBA Group Super - Accumulate Plus	12.8	6.4	6.9	6.3	7.2
EISS Super	17.7	7.1	7.4	6.9	7.4
Energy Super	17.7	6.4	7.9	7.6	
Equip MyFuture	16.4	7.5	8.5	7.8	
First Super - Employer Sponsored	14.3	6.2	8.0		8.0
GESB Super	16.7	7.0	7.4		7.6
GuildSuper	25.5	10.3	9.7	8.4	
HESTA	18.8	8.3	9.2	8.3	8.7
Hostplus	21.2	8.2	10.0	9.3	9.5

Annual average investment returns, net of all fees, 30 June, 2021

MySuper product name	1 year	3 years	5 years	7 years	10 years
Intrust Super - Core Super	16.9	6.9	8.6	8.1	8.5
IOOF Employer Super - Employer	16.3	7.9	8.3		
legalsuper	16.8	7.6	8.4	7.8	8.2
LGIAsuper Accumulation	15.0	7.1	8.1		7.9
LUCRF Super	18.3	7.3	8.1	7.2	7.6
Lutheran Super	16.8	8.6	9.3		
Media Super	16.7	8.1	9.1	8.2	8.3
Mercer Super Trust - Corporate	21.8	8.8	9.5		
Mercy Super	15.9	7.4	8.9	8.1	8.6
NGS Super Accumulation	17.2	7.6	8.8	8.0	7.9
Prime Super	18.1	7.9	9.0	8.5	8.8
PSS accumulation plan	18.2	8.0	8.5	8.0	8.4
Qantas Super Gateway	26.5	9.8	10.4		
QSuper Accumulation Account	16.9	8.8	8.4	9.1	
REI Super	19.6	7.0	7.3	7.3	7.9
Rest Super	17.2	6.9	8.0	7.2	8.1
smartMonday PRIME	20.7	9.0	10.0		
Spirit Super	17.1	7.5	8.5	8.4	7.9
StatewideSuper	18.0	7.5	8.9	8.7	
Sunsuper for Life Business	20.3	8.5	9.5	8.6	8.8
Telstra Super Corporate Plus	24.6	9.5	10.3	8.9	9.6
TWUSUPER	18.8	7.4	8.3	7.6	8.2
UniSuper	17.4	9.0	9.4	9.0	9.4
VicSuper FutureSaver	18.2	8.8	9.2	8.3	8.8
Virgin Money Super Employer	22.0	10.0			
Vision Super Saver	18.8	8.9	9.7	8.5	8.7
VISSF Accumulation	20.4	7.9			
Max	**26.5**	**10.3**	**10.6**	**9.4**	**9.6**
Median	**17.9**	**7.9**	**8.7**	**8.3**	**8.3**
Min	**12.8**	**6.2**	**6.9**	**6.3**	**7.2**

As at June 30, 2021. Only MySuper products quality assessed as AAA by Rainmaker Information are included in this table. Investment returns are net of all fees that are applicable to a $50,000 account balance, including member fees.

Insurance through your super

MySuper products and super funds use their group buying power to offer members insurance at wholesale prices. But how do you know if your fund's insurance policy is any good?

KEY POINTS

- Insurance offered by your MySuper product or super fund can be cheaper because your fund groups its members under a single wholesale insurance policy.

- Insurance bought through your fund is held in the name of the super fund trustees, so it's different to normal insurance policies that you hold directly in your name.

- Your super fund gets a tax refund equivalent to 15% of the premiums you have paid for your insurance cover. Funds use this refund to either reduce your net premiums, reduce the fees they have to charge you, or to defray other fund operating expenses.

Insurance is a big deal when selecting a super fund or a MySuper product because many of them use their buying power to obtain insurance at wholesale group rates that can often be cheaper than if you purchased the same insurance cover yourself at the regular rates you'd have to pay as a private individual.

Buying insurance through your super fund has other advantages too: because the premium prices – the amount you pay for your insurance, sometimes called the insurance fee – are taken out of your pre-tax super contributions, it is effectively paid through your employer so you don't have to send the insurance company a cheque each month from your take-home pay.

Group insurance

Super funds and MySuper products can offer these insurance deals because they group their members together into very large, combined wholesale insurance policies. This enables them to buy insurance at cheaper rates because large groups of super fund members are insured under a single insurance policy held in the name of the super fund's trustees. Even better, insurance you buy through your super fund is free of any sales commissions, although some super funds might charge you insurance administration fees.

These super fund group insurance policies can also be simpler than regular insurance because they are usually based solely on the member's age or other overall characteristics of the group. Some super funds may, however, split members into higher-risk or lower-risk occupational groups, e.g., trades workers versus executive managers, heavy blue-collar versus light manual, and white-collar versus professional. By choosing the right occupational risk grouping super funds are able to offer insurance at the lowest premium prices they can.

Types of insurance
Life insurance you buy through your super fund usually comes in three main types:

1. Death only
This pays your nominated beneficiary a set amount upon your death.

2. Death and total and permanent disability (death/TPD)
This is the most common type of insurance you can get through your superannuation. It includes death-only insurance but you may also be able to claim against your insurance policy if you are catastrophically injured or cannot work again because of a disability, subject to the policy's terms and conditions. If you make a TPD claim, upon your death your insurance cover reduces to the balance of the overall insured amount not already paid.

3. Income protection (IP)
This is sometimes also called salary continuance insurance, **sickness and accident insurance** or temporary **disability insurance**. If you cannot work because of injury or temporary disability, you may be able to claim part of your lost salary while you recover.

Some funds may also offer home and contents insurance and health insurance, though this is usually done through the fund obtaining a special deal with an insurance company, so you get the insurance at a discount. While not many super funds currently offer these arrangements, they are gradually becoming more common.

Standard insurance cover

When you join a MySuper product or a super fund you usually have to buy a minimum level of insurance cover. The graph below shows standard death and TPD cover.

This **standard cover** is usually combined Death and TPD cover although some funds also include income protection cover. The level of this cover in 2021 averaged up to $200,000 for an average premium of $6.25 per week if you were 40 years of age. Note, however, that the range of insurance can vary significantly between funds, e.g., some funds offer almost $450,000 in standard cover.

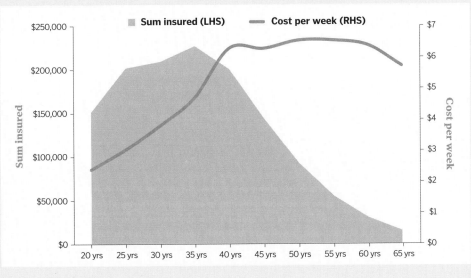

Source: Rainmaker Information

Insurance for young people or those with a low account balance

If you are younger than 25 years of age or have super account balance under $6,000, you no longer have to purchase your fund's standard cover insurance. But you can opt-in if you wish.

Binding beneficiaries

One thing to remember when buying insurance through your MySuper product or super fund is that because the trustees hold the policy rather than you, if you or your estate ever have to make a claim, the trustees are obliged to check that the person making the claim is doing so legitimately, i.e., it has to be paid to a **dependant**. Trustees have to make these judgments – it's part of their job – but unfortunately this can sometimes slow down the payment process.

To minimise the chance of this happening, many super funds have introduced **binding beneficiary** nominations. These guide the fund into paying the insurance benefit to a specific **dependant** person nominated by the deceased super fund member. However, if you want your super death benefits to be paid to someone else, you should nominate your estate as your binding beneficiary and be sure your **will** explains that you want them to receive this money.

Automatic acceptance limits (AALs)

Super funds that offer large choices of insurance usually have pre-set maximums for how much insurance members can buy without needing to undergo a medical assessment. These maximum amounts are referred to as **automatic acceptance limits** (AALs).

For example, your fund may have an AAL of $500,000, which means you can get $500,000 in insurance cover without having to answer more

detailed questions or submit to a medical examination – a process called underwriting.

The premium rates for cover above the AAL are nearly always the same as for below-AAL cover, so in many ways the AAL in itself is not really a big deal. Still, in order to access more insurance cover than stipulated by the AAL, you may have to undergo a medical assessment. The problem is that doing this could raise the risk of you being refused insurance cover if a major medical problem is found.

However, where AALs are a big issue is when companies transfer their super into a new super fund. This is because sometimes the AALs are based on a predetermined proportion – say 75% – of all the company's employees taking up the insurance offer. This means if not enough employees take up the offer, then the AALs may not apply as generously as first thought and all members may even need to undertake medical assessments. This could lead to the premiums going up.

Claims experience

While all insurance policies may appear similar, figures published by the superannuation regulator APRA have shown that there are large differences between insurers regarding how quickly they pay claims. For example, it takes on average one month for insurers to process death claims, six months to process TPD claims and two months to process income protection claims. However, some insurers have been found to take much longer.

Consumer warning: policy terms & conditions

Choosing the right insurance is not just about price; you should also check the policy terms and conditions. This matters because funds' policies can have subtly different definitions of what they call a disability. For example, if you are catastrophically injured some policies may pay you out if you can't do your current job, but others may only pay you out if you cannot do any job for which the insurer thinks you could be suitable. The tighter the definition, however, the cheaper your insurance premiums should be – which is why some super funds, in an effort to keep their premiums low, are doing this.

Insurance alert when changing funds

Group insurance through your MySuper product or super fund can save you money, but the insurance is only very rarely transferable to other super funds. This means if you are thinking of changing super funds and you want insurance as part of your new super fund, you must first check if the new super fund's insurance is as good as the insurance of your current super fund.

So, if under super choice you are tempted to change super funds and you have insurance through your current super fund, please first check the insurance arrangements of the new fund before doing anything. In fact, if you are over age 40 and have insurance through your super fund, you should be 100% certain that the new fund will accept you for insurance. If you have the slightest doubt, then get a written promise from the new fund that it will offer you a policy.

How to compare insurance premiums

There are two main methods super funds use to describe how they calculate their insurance premium rates:

- **The unit-price method –** A member buys predefined amounts of insurance cover for a set premium per unit; e.g., $70,000 cover (sum insured) for $1 per week. Members can then buy more insurance cover simply by buying more units.
- **The fixed-price method –** Members can buy whatever amount of insurance they like, and the premium is derived by multiplying the price per $1,000 of cover by how many thousands of dollars in cover you want e.g., for every $1,000 in insurance cover you pay 74c a year, so $300,000 cover costs 74c x 300, which is $222 per year.

The unit-price method used to be most widely used by in-house corporate, public sector and industry super funds, while the fixed-price method used to be most widely used by retail super funds. Many funds now, however, offer their insurance using both pricing methods. A trick to watch for when comparing insurance policies is whether the premiums are described in per week, per month or per annum terms. It's not always as clear as it should be.

Another thing to watch if a super fund offers its insurance using both premium methods is that the premium deals are not always in sync,

so you may end up paying higher premiums just because you chose the wrong payment calculation method.

For income protection insurance, you also need to consider:

- **The waiting period –** how long you have to be sick until you can apply for your benefit. The most common waiting periods are 30 days and 90 days, though some funds use 45 days and some funds use six-month waiting periods. The general rule is that the longer the waiting period, the cheaper the insurance premiums.
- **The benefit period –** how long your benefits will be paid until you have to apply for a full TPD payout, assuming you have TPD insurance. Most superannuation fund insurance policies have a two-year benefit period, though a very small number have benefit periods that extend up until your normally expected retirement age of 55 to 65. Normal income protection insurance bought directly from an insurance company has this extended benefit period as standard.

Income protection premiums paid through your super fund are sometimes tax deductible for a short time, depending upon your individual circumstances, though for many people they are not normally tax deductible by you. This is because your super fund has already claimed a tax deduction for buying the insurance policy.

MySuper products with best value insurance 2021

The table below describes the premium value of the standard insurance default cover available through different MySuper products where this is defined as insurance cover (sum insured) per dollar of weekly premium paid. MySuper products offering the best value are those with the highest values.

| MySuper product | Insurance cover per $ weekly premium | | | |
| | Death and TPD | | Monthly income protection | |
	Low risk	High risk	Low risk	High risk
Active Super Accumulation Scheme	37,572	23,483	1,270	847
AMG Corporate Super	65,632	37,410	1,429	643
AMIST Super Employer	24,520	16,346	1,250	909
ANZ Staff Super - Employee	59,091			
ANZ Smart Choice Super - Employer	41,600	12,235	1,499	681
Australian Catholic - Employer	54,167		455	
ADF Super	18,182		531	
Australian Ethical Super	59,091	29,545	733	333
AustralianSuper	34,843	19,157	735	476
AvSuper Corporate	80,833	31,699	893	313
Aware Super - Employer Sponsored	65,823	29,885	1,128	594
Bendigo SmartStart - Employer	43,400	27,125	940	537
BUSSQ MySuper	45,045	19,920		
CareSuper	28,430	24,919	903	602
Catholic Super	65,823		1,174	
CBA Group Super - Accumulate Plus	58,427		1,166	
Cbus Industry Super	26,299	16,883	985	
Christian Super	53,378	28,214		
Club Plus Industry Division		38,023		
EISS Super	38,012	23,392	1,126	643
Energy Super	42,003	33,592		
Equip MyFuture	144,444	52,000		1,200
First Super - Employer Sponsored	26,396	12,235	747	270
CFS - FirstChoice Employer Super	32,911	16,456	1,323	662
GESB Super	37,741	29,140	607	289
GuildSuper	36,620	25,243		
HESTA	37,175	26,110	291	204

	Insurance cover per $ weekly premium			
	Death and TPD		**Monthly income protection**	
MySuper product	**Low risk**	**High risk**	**Low risk**	**High risk**
Hostplus	33,987	12,536	823	257
Intrust Super - Core Super		44,379		779
IOOF Employer Super - Employer	33,333	19,608	679	340
legalsuper	43,297		922	
LGIAsuper Accumulation	37,956	27,807	874	655
LUCRF Super	37,143	22,807	1,380	786
Lutheran Super	75,362			
Maritime Super	63,000	26,000	1,181	336
Media Super	48,950			
Mercy Super	106,159	37,432	868	397
NGS Super Accumulation	64,677	29,083		
Prime Super	65,000	26,131	972	389
PSS accumulation plan	30,233		688	
Qantas Super Gateway	35,326	17,663		
QSuper Accumulation Account	30,534	19,847	253	177
REI Super	39,394		561	
Rest Super	35,750	20,854		
smartMonday PRIME	51,485	30,233	837	431
Spirit Super	21,136	16,099	612	429
StatewideSuper	43,189	23,996		
Sunsuper for Life Business		73,239	1,376	
Telstra Super Corporate Plus	45,217	22,609	926	370
TWUSUPER	45,455	12,346	885	291
UniSuper	78,788		1,260	
VicSuper FutureSaver	37,956	30,409	413	391
Virgin Money Super Employer	95,378	37,117		
Vision Super Saver	50,980			633
VISSF Accumulation	58,231			
Max	**144,444**	**73,239**	**1,813**	**2,203**
Median	**42,276**	**25,266**	**948**	**542**
Min	**18,182**	**787**	**253**	**177**

Insurance rates vary by risk category of the member. Income protection insurance premium also varies by waiting period. This tables assumes member age of 40 and income protection with 30-day waiting period and 2-year benefit period.

Super fund fees

To understand how much you are really paying in superannuation fees, you have to demystify the different ways products and funds describe them.

KEY POINTS

- The more fees you pay, the higher your investment returns must be to make up for them.

- While there are many types of fees, you can group them together to derive your overall total expense ratio.

- Fees are now capped at 3% if your account balance is less than $6,000, while exit fees are now banned.

Your aim in selecting a MySuper product or superannuation fund is to find one that will make you as financially independent as possible by the time you retire or leave the workforce, without exposing you to too much unnecessary investment risk along the way. To do this, your super fund must earn consistently strong rates of investment returns net of fees – year in, year out.

Fees affect your investment returns

To give you a better chance of building your retirement savings, it helps if your MySuper product or super fund charges only low or reasonable fees. Why? Because what you get in your pocket is what's left from the investment returns after all the fees are taken out; – it is as simple as that. So the higher the fees, the higher the returns have to be to leave you with more money in your pocket.

An example will highlight why this is so important to understand. If two 20-year-old super fund members achieve identical investment returns but one pays only 1% in fees each year while the other pays 2% in fees each year, the member in the higher-fee fund will retire with 20% less. This impact is shown in the graphs later in this chapter.

So paying higher fees can cost you big money. And this means that if you are paying higher fees you should make sure you use the fund shrewdly, so that you more than make up for these fees through better investment mixes and higher returns.

All about the fees

When checking out superannuation fees, there are three main types you should know about, as shown in detail in the table at the end of this article. These are:

- **Administration fees** are paid to your superannuation fund to cover its regulatory, administration, platform, compliance, technology and marketing costs.
- **Investment fees** are paid to your fund's investment managers and asset consultants. These fees might also be called the indirect cost ratio.
- **Member fees** are also paid to your super fund, usually to cover account keeping.

Some funds used to also charge contribution fees, also known as entry fees, that were paid to financial advisers when you join the fund. But because advisers can no longer receive commissions from superannuation products, these fees are rarely charged nowadays.

These fee types mean that the different people involved with your super are getting a different share of your fees. For example, in many super funds, the investment managers may be receiving two-thirds of the fees you are paying. Some funds may also bundle their management and investment fees into a larger combined figure, meaning that if your fund reports a zero investment fee it doesn't mean it is investing your superannuation for free; it instead just means it has structured its arrangements differently.

You can often get discounts on this fee if you ask for it or if you are contributing a large amount of money into your superannuation fund.

When working out your total fees, don't forget to also count the member fee. If you are starting out in super, this member fee is your biggest headache and funds that might at first seem expensive can sometimes actually be cheaper for you because they don't charge a member fee. For example, if you have only $1,000 in your fund, a $1.50 per week member fee is costing you $78 per year. This converts to 7.8% of your account which is likely to be five times the combined management and investment fees. Of course, these ratios change quickly as your account balance grows.

There are also some tricks of the trade you should watch for when it comes to fees and charges. For example, some products or funds claim to have low or even zero fees, even though they make this happen by deducting extra costs from their earnings rates before declaring your crediting rate.

Watch out especially for funds that try to confuse you by talking about fees charged to the fund and how they are different to fees charged directly to you. Anything that comes off the top of your return before you receive it is a fee to you – no ifs, no buts.

Indirect cost ratio

Some super funds no longer declare investment fees instead referring to their indirect cost ratio (ICR). They use this term because these charges may not be paid directly by the fund but indirectly by members. For example, the investment manager deducts their share of the ICR fee from the gross investment return they achieve before declaring their net investment return that they pass onto the fund. In cases where an administration fee is bundled with an investment fee, the ICR may replace both of these. When you see an ICR, just think of it as a percentage fee that applies to your account balance.

Calculating your super fees

A fee calculation converts all the fees you are paying into a single dollar amount.

It then applies that amount to your overall account balance to come up with your total fee as a percentage of your account balance. We call this percentage your **total expense ratio**, or TER.

Knowing the different fees charged by different products and super funds means you can calculate the different TERs. It is important to realise, however, that a TER does not indicate the future performance of a fund – but we do know that higher fees rarely lead to better investment returns. Proving this, many of Australia's top-performing MySuper products and super funds usually have low fees anyway, so why pay higher fees if you don't have to?

For most members with $50,000 or more in super, the biggest fee culprit is the administration fee because it is usually the highest, while the fee with least impact is the member fee (once your account balance grows) because the $1.50 per week converts to only 0.16% on a $50,000 account balance. The member fee, however, has a bigger impact when you're starting out in superannuation and you have a smaller account balance.

As a result of this, if you want to receive a deal on your super fund fees, you will get the best results if you dial down the management fees. It is, of course, good if you can dial down other fees, but it's the

Fees capped at 3%, exit fees banned

Fees are now capped at 3% if you have less than $6,000 in your super fund account, and exit fees are banned. But this doesn't mean funds charge less than 3% in fees. Instead, at the end of each year if you have less than $6,000 in your account they will refund any fees you have paid above this 3% limit.

Impact of fees upon your end retirement benefit

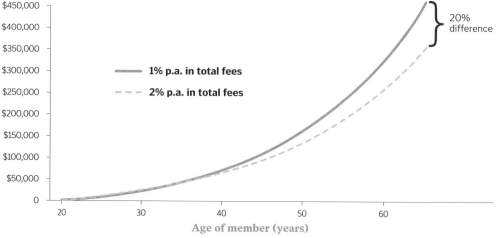

Source: Rainmaker Information

management fees that you should worry about first.

While the average superannuation member across Australia pays a TER of about 1%, this covers everybody whether they are in SMSFs, public sector schemes, not-for-profit and retail funds. A better comparison is that if you are in an industry or retail fund and paying less than 1%, you are in a very sharply priced fund, while if you are paying between 1% and 1.2% you are paying a reasonable price.

New laws passed in 2019 banned super funds from charging fees above 3% if you have less than $6,000 in your super fund account and also banned exit fees. To comply with this new 3% fee cap, super funds aren't necessarily lowering their fees but at the end of each year if you have less than $6,000 in your account they will refund any fees you have paid above the 3% threshold.

Some workplace retail funds, such as corporate master trusts, meanwhile, can sharpen their fee deals for some client companies so much that there may be hardly any difference between their fees and those of a low-cost industry fund. This is because most corporate master trusts will negotiate on fees, and if you represent a company or you have a sizeable amount of superannuation in your company account you should never be afraid to bargain hard for a better deal.

Reflecting this, simple comparisons of the fee rates don't always tell the whole story.

To calculate your fund's TER follow this example

Step 1	What is your administration fee?	0.50%
Step 2	What is your investment fee?	0.00%
	Or, what is your investment's indirect cost ratio?	0.65%
	What performance fee did you pay?	0.10%
Step 3	What is your member fee per year (e.g., $1.50 per week x 52 = $78)?	$78
	Divide this figure by $50,000	0.00156
	Multiply your answer by 100	0.16%
Step 4	Add the percentages together – this is your total expense ratio.	1.41%

Congratulations!
You have just calculated your total expense ratio and are now a super fund fee expert. Well done.

Super fund fee types

Description	Applies to?	Who gets it?	What's normal?	Negotiable?
Administration How much it costs to stay in the fund. Sometimes also called plan management or administration fees.	Account balance	The fund, but sometimes shared with the adviser	Up to 2%	Sometimes
Investment How much you have to pay your investment manager(s). Some funds now refer to this as the indirect cost ratio	Account balance	The investment manager	Up to 1% p.a.	Not usually
Member How much you pay for account-keeping and basic administration of your account.	Flat dollar fee	The fund	Up to $80 p.a.	Not usually

MySuper AAA product fees 2021

The table below describes the fee deals available through different MySuper products.

Product name	Product fees		Investment fees & costs		
	Member fee $ p.a.	Ongoing fee % p.a.	Investment fee % p.a.	Indirect cost ratio	TER
Active Super Accumulation Scheme	71.24	0.25%	0.33%	0.47%	1.19%
AMG Corporate Super	65.00	0.41%	0.12%	0.04%	0.70%
AMIST Super Employer	88.70	0.07%	0.56%	0.00%	0.81%
ANZ Staff Super - Employee	0.00	0.08%	0.00%	0.50%	0.58%
ANZ Smart Choice Super - Employer	60.00	0.23%	0.60%	0.07%	1.02%
Australian Catholic - Employer	78.00	0.25%	0.38%	0.33%	1.12%
ADF Super	84.00	0.00%	0.00%	1.15%	1.32%
Australian Ethical Super	97.00	0.29%	0.64%	0.12%	1.24%
AustralianSuper	117.00	0.04%	0.50%	0.00%	0.77%
AvSuper Corporate	59.80	0.19%	0.73%	0.17%	1.21%
Aware Super - Employer Sponsored	52.00	0.15%	0.74%	0.00%	0.99%
Bendigo SmartStart - Employer	98.04	0.00%	0.00%	0.50%	0.70%
BT Super	108.00	0.28%	0.50%	0.16%	1.16%
BUSSQ MySuper	117.00	0.00%	0.00%	1.04%	1.27%
CareSuper	78.00	0.19%	0.24%	0.50%	1.09%
Catholic Super	93.60	0.18%	0.83%	0.17%	1.37%
CBA Group Super - Accumulate Plus	77.65	0.17%	0.50%	0.00%	0.83%
Cbus Industry Super	104.00	0.19%	0.56%	0.00%	0.96%
Christian Super	65.00	0.27%	0.38%	0.51%	1.29%
Club Plus Industry Division	93.60	0.20%	0.87%	0.00%	1.26%
EISS Super	0.00	0.39%	0.26%	0.24%	0.89%
Energy Super	52.00	0.18%	0.35%	0.38%	1.01%
Equip MyFuture	52.00	0.25%	0.32%	0.29%	0.96%
First Super - Employer Sponsored	117.00	0.20%	0.68%	0.04%	1.15%
CFS - FirstChoice Employer Super	60.00	0.30%	0.40%	0.08%	0.90%
GESB Super	66.00	0.20%	0.00%	0.49%	0.82%
GuildSuper	115.00	0.15%	0.60%	0.19%	1.17%
HESTA	65.00	0.08%	0.73%	0.09%	1.03%
Hostplus	78.00	0.00%	0.71%	0.39%	1.26%
Intrust Super - Core Super	78.00	0.30%	0.77%	0.00%	1.23%

Product name	Product fees		Investment fees & costs		
	Member fee $ p.a.	Ongoing fee % p.a.	Investment fee % p.a.	Indirect cost ratio	TER
IOOF Employer Super - Employer	117.00	0.35%	0.00%	0.50%	1.08%
legalsuper	67.60	0.29%	0.62%	0.20%	1.25%
LGIAsuper Accumulation	52.00	0.18%	0.48%	0.69%	1.45%
LUCRF Super	78.00	0.18%	0.25%	0.30%	0.89%
Lutheran Super	91.00	0.30%	0.59%	0.00%	1.07%
Maritime Super	65.00	0.22%	0.71%	0.39%	1.45%
Media Super	65.00	0.15%	0.22%	0.47%	0.97%
Mercer Super Trust - Corporate	91.68	0.40%	0.44%	0.36%	1.38%
Mercy Super	0.00	0.25%	0.84%	0.00%	1.09%
NGS Super Accumulation	65.00	0.10%	0.62%	0.07%	0.92%
Prime Super	67.60	0.00%	0.50%	0.51%	1.15%
PSS accumulation plan	84.00	0.00%	0.00%	1.15%	1.32%
Qantas Super Gateway	98.00	0.24%	0.39%	0.56%	1.39%
QSuper Accumulation Account	0.00	0.16%	0.45%	0.13%	0.74%
REI Super	85.80	0.25%	0.58%	0.12%	1.12%
Rest Super	78.00	0.12%	0.55%	0.06%	0.89%
smartMonday PRIME	72.00	0.44%	0.38%	0.07%	1.03%
Spirit Super	67.60	0.15%	0.74%	0.00%	1.03%
StatewideSuper	91.00	0.11%	0.85%	0.00%	1.14%
Sunsuper for Life Business	78.00	0.10%	0.27%	0.41%	0.94%
Telstra Super Corporate Plus	78.00	0.18%	0.84%	0.00%	1.18%
TWUSUPER	78.00	0.25%	0.17%	0.55%	1.13%
UniSuper	96.00	0.00%	0.40%	0.06%	0.65%
VicSuper FutureSaver	52.00	0.15%	0.73%	0.00%	0.98%
Virgin Money Super Employer	58.00	0.39%	0.12%	0.10%	0.73%
Vision Super Saver	78.00	0.14%	0.54%	0.09%	0.93%
VISSF Accumulation	52.00	0.00%	0.73%	0.32%	1.15%
Max	**150.00**	**0.70%**	**1.13%**	**1.22%**	**1.60%**
Median	**78.00**	**0.18%**	**0.47%**	**0.25%**	**1.08%**
Min	**0.00**	**0.00%**	**0.00%**	**0.00%**	**0.63%**

Only MySuper products quality assessed by Rainmaker Information as AAA are included in this table. Product fees is the addition of member fees, applicable to a $50,000 account balance, and ongoing administration fees. Total expense ratio (TER) is the addition of both product and investment fees and costs.

Extra benefits available

Many MySuper products and super funds do more than just help you save for retirement. Most also offer insurance and financial advice and some offer home loans, health insurance and shopping deals.

The job of your MySuper product or super fund is making money for you and the other members. But super funds can do more for their members than just that so you don't have to wait until you retire before you can start getting something back.

They do this by setting up strategic partnerships and alliances with insurers, banks, financial advisers, travel companies and other product providers. Some super funds have so many features it makes them almost one-stop-financial-shops.

The battle for your loyalty that this race has ignited is so intense that some funds are updating their list of product features and offerings nearly every month.

Latest research

To find out what funds offer which extra features, Rainmaker Information analyses the incidence of over 50 individual features and benefits offerings across more than 500 superannuation and retirement products annually.

Rainmaker Information regularly finds that the extra features funds offer range from call centres to online account access, insurance, smart phone and tablet apps, financial products like home loans, shopping rewards, social media presence and even shopping discounts like health insurance, travel deals and gym memberships.

But while features such as being online, having a call centre, life insurance, financial planning services or retirement products are offered by almost every super fund, other features like shopping and travel discounts and general insurance are offered by only a few funds.

So the message is clear: not all funds offer everything so if there's something special you want, you have to compare your fund in detail.

This race to have lots of product features is why the average number of features offered by funds has increased year on year and now stands at over 20, with the feature types growing the fastest being technology-based communications and those features that reflect increased member engagement

in investments and information about your portfolios.

An increasing number of super funds are offering access to cash term deposits within investment choice menus, regular investment reports and online investment switching. This follows the growing interaction between super funds and their members regarding how the assets are invested and managed, although these features can at times make funds seem unnecessarily complex.

These, coupled with the increase in transaction functionality (e.g., EFT/BPAY contributions, online account access, apps for mobile devices), also reflect this increased technology focus, notwithstanding it's still surprising how few super funds have their own smartphone apps.

However, not all features and benefits are valued equally by all members, so just because a fund has lots of product features doesn't mean it's the best superannuation fund – recall that the most important feature for your fund will always be delivering the best investment returns that it can.

MDI options

Member direct investment (MDI) options are like mini investment platforms that give super fund members direct access to the ASX 300, exchange traded funds (ETFs), term deposits and listed investment companies (LICs).

Around 30% of workplace funds offer these options with a relatively even split between not-for-profit and retail funds. Almost half of all super funds now offer cash term deposits.

Investment switching

If you are a fund member who likes to switch investments, make sure to check for funds that offer unlimited switches, that promise to do it quickly or that at least give you a reasonable number of free switches before they start charging you. Not all funds want you to switch investment choices too often, so be careful to check the fine print if this is a feature that's important to you.

Extra benefits and MySuper

If you join a direct, low-cost, standalone MySuper product, it is unlikely to offer you many extra benefits. If you want access to these extra benefits you should instead join a regular super fund that contains a MySuper option because the extra benefits are available across the fund even if the member uses only the MySuper option.

Extra features available through super funds

Member services	Account flexibility
Website	Retirement products
Online account access	EFT/BPAY contributions
Call centre	Spouse accounts
Newsletters for members	Transition to retirement facility
Education seminars	Contribution splitting
Newsletters for employers	Binding death benefit nominations
Mobile website or app	Anti-detriment payments
Social media presence	Can handle defined benefit arrangements
Online membership application	Linked account fee discounting
Webchat	Can join without employer
	Children's super accounts
	Home saver accounts

Investment flexibility	Ancillary services
Investment choice	Non-super investment products
Multi-manager investment choice(s)	Home loans
Online investment switching	Personal loans
Monthly or quarterly investment reports	Credit cards
Choice of asset allocation	Savings account
Ethical/SRI investment choice(s)	Insurance – private health
Term deposit investment choice	Business loans
Choice of fund managers	Insurance – travel
Age-based investment choice	Shopping discounts
Automatic portfolio rebalancing	Insurance – car
Direct shares investment facility	Travel discounts
Dollar cost averaging investment plan	Insurance – home (building)
	Insurance – home (contents)

Life insurance options	Financial advice
Insurance – death and TPD	Financial advice – limited
Insurance – death only	Financial advice – full financial planning
Insurance – income protection	Robo or online advice

KEY POINTS

- Super funds do much more than just look after your superannuation. Most also offer insurance, financial advice, online account access, retirement products, home loans, non-super investments, access to direct shares and even shopping discounts

- But their main job will still always be delivering long-term investment returns.

- When choosing your super fund, look for funds with the best investment outcomes then worry about the extras.

Super and young people

Most super funds have been designed for older people with high account balances, not young people who are just starting out in superannuation.

KEY POINTS

- When you're starting out in superannuation, fees matter more than performance.

- Look for percentage fees that are less than 1% p.a.

- Watch out for funds that charge dollar-based membership fees.

- Insurance will cost you more than your regular fees. If you're young and don't need it, think hard before agreeing to buy it.

When you're young and just starting your working life, superannuation and your future retirement will probably be the last thing on your mind. You won't be too worried about your choice of super fund and you'll be quite happy to join the one you're told to join or one with a high profile brand that you like.

If you're lucky, this can be a good strategy – you'll join a good-value, strongly performing super fund that offers great product features. But not everyone is so lucky. To ensure you get off to a good start in your superannuation life, there's a few things to know:

1. superannuation is compulsory for most people, and it's your money; and
2. a super fund is just a savings account purpose-built to help you save for your retirement.

Fees matter more to young people

Super funds charge fees that are a combination of percentage-based investment and administration fees charged against your account balance and a flat dollar-based member fee.

In 2021, default MySuper products charged an average fee of 1.1%, made up of 0.16% p.a. for administration, 0.7% p.a. for investment management and $70 p.a. for member fees. Administration and member fees counted together are also called product fees.

But when Rainmaker Information and people in the superannuation industry talk about fees, they usually mean the fees that apply to people with $50,000 in their account. When you're young and starting out, you won't have $50,000, but probably only a few hundred or maybe a thousand dollars.

If this is you, you could be paying actual fees of 10% or more. Even though fees above 3% will now be refunded to you at the end of each year, this means that the money you've paid in these high fees wasn't being invested for you. In any case, why pay high fees if you don't have to?

Because of this, young people often pay fees that are about eight times more than the 1.1% average paid by older people.

Super and young people

There are 3.3 million people in Australia aged between 15 and 24 who have 2.7 million superannuation accounts worth $14 billion. But a better way to look at this is that these young people hold 12% of all the member accounts but only 1% of the money – which is why many super funds don't focus enough on the needs of their young members. But down the track, you will need to focus on your financial needs, and if your super fund treats you badly now, it will most likely treat you badly when you do have money. Don't cop it; swap funds.

Signs you're in a good super fund

- **Trust.** You trust the organisation and the people who run the fund and its superannuation products.

- **Performance.** The investment options you intend using achieve above-average returns over the medium term, e.g., over three or five years.

- **Fees.** It charges good-value fees around 1% p.a. or less. If your fund is charging higher fees, you should be getting something special; remember, to justify paying higher fees, your investment returns have to be even higher so that you can make back the difference.

Insurance and the total cost of super

Members who are under age 25 don't have to buy compulsory life insurance through their super fund. Once you are 25 and over, if you are a member of a MySuper product, you do have to, even though you can choose to opt-out (cancel it) at any time. This life insurance can be a mix of death insurance, total and permanent disability insurance and income protection insurance.

While this insurance is cheap in overall terms, averaging $130 p.a. for $230,000 cover if you are aged 25, if you have $5,000 in your super account it converts to 2.6% of your account balance. Adding this insurance fee to the regular fees means that you are now paying 6% p.a. in total fees.

But the scary part is that if you are just starting out and have only about $1,000 in superannuation, you could be paying total regular fees and insurance fees equivalent to 25% of your account balance. The chart shows you how this works.

The point we are trying to highlight to young people is that while Australia has a lot of very good super funds that will earn you good investment returns and provide you with great deals on insurance, most of these funds have been designed for older people who have more money in their accounts.

Young people need to look at their superannuation a bit differently.

Features all good funds should have

Every smart, modern super fund should have a good website with lots of useful, easy-to-understand information, online account access, be easy to deal with and most likely have a smartphone app. But this doesn't matter much if you don't trust the fund, if its performance isn't any good and it's expensive.

Your total fees as your account balance gets bigger

Chart shows the average fees you will pay depending on your account balance. It assumes you are age 25 and have to buy compulsory insurance.

Regular fees   **Insurance fees**

Source: Rainmaker Information

How to compare MySuper products and funds

Kicking the tyres of a MySuper product or super fund is easy if you know how.

KEY POINTS

- Not all super funds are the same. They can offer different features best suited for particular types of members.

- Comparing super funds feature by feature will help you decide which fund is best for you.

The challenge for anyone choosing a MySuper product or super fund, whether you are an employer, employee or an individual looking for a personal superannuation product, is to find one that suits you. This is because not all products and funds are the same as they are designed to serve the needs of different types of members. For example, some are aimed at people who want simple, low-cost super, some are aimed at people who want lots of choices and some are aimed at people who want direct access to their own investments.

To sort out which superannuation funds and products will suit you, the challenge is to figure out what they offer, what features you like, which are likely to deliver you the best investment returns for the most reasonable fees, and which have the best insurance deals.

Recall that your superannuation account is really not that different to any other savings account you have, except that your superannuation account is one you will have your whole working life and probably throughout your retirement. That is, a young person joining the workforce this year could be a member of that product or fund for up to 70 years.

What makes a superannuation account different is its purpose; you are not saving for day-to-day expenses or even a car or a holiday, but for your retirement. Its primary purpose is building up a large enough account balance to fund your retirement income.

Super funds and products achieve this by making smart investment decisions, either themselves or in consultation with their own advisers, and by utilising the services of quality investment managers who then invest the fund's money on behalf of the members to earn good rates of return. The icing on the cake is that along the way they may also give great online account access, good deals on insurance, access to other investment products and banking services, financial advice and even shopping discounts.

What features to compare

A good way to understand any super fund is to look at it as a collection of features centred around investments, insurance and account access. When you do this you will realise the smart way to compare any super fund is to look at its investment choices, its investment return track records, fees, insurance packages and other features like its online account access, availability of good-quality financial advice through the fund and whether it offers other financial products like banking, loans, credit cards or savings plans.

Comparing investment options may seem daunting, but all you need to do is check whether the investment returns from the main options are above or below average over the medium term, say three, five or 10 years. You should also look at the total fees your fund charges, noting that anything above 1% is now considered highly priced. And then you should find out what types of insurance packages are available and what they cost.

If you want direct control over your investments, you should also check whether you're able to invest directly into particular companies listed on the ASX and also exchange traded funds, listed investment companies or cash term deposits.

Good super funds and products are also transparent and open about how they invest your money, which means they provide clear information describing the investment managers they use and what underlying shares and debt securities they invest in – this last aspect is called portfolio holdings disclosure. If you want your superannuation invested into things like renewable energy, this is especially important for you to know.

Other investment questions to ask are: can you choose indexed investments, ethically managed investments, and an age-based lifecycle strategy? Several super funds also provide discounted access to health insurance, so you should check whether your fund does as well.

How to compare investment returns

- Check out your super fund's returns by visiting moneymag.com.au/super/funds/compare.
- Select the table for MySuper options or the asset class you are comparing.
- Looking at investment returns over the medium term, say three, five or 10 years, is your fund achieving about average or better? If it is, it's a good returner. If it's in the top 10 or 20 even better.

KEY POINTS

- Investment returns, insurance premium prices and fees are the most important features to compare.

- Employers can pay members' default contributions only into a MySuper product or a super fund that contains a MySuper option.

You can't join every product or fund

When you start looking for a MySuper product or super fund to join, you will quickly realise you can't join every product or fund because not all are open to every employer, every employee or the general public. For example, it may be open to only public sector employees, or an in-house corporate fund will only be open to employees of that company.

As a result, for most people this means you will really be choosing between MySuper products and super funds offered by corporate or personal master trust operators or by industry funds. Note that some public offer public sector funds now qualify as industry funds.

Direct or through a financial adviser?

A good way to understand your MySuper product or super fund is to look at how you can join it. For example, can you join it directly over the internet, do you have to join through your employer, or do you have to go through an intermediary such as a financial adviser?

This matters because products or funds you can join directly are usually cheaper because they tend to be simpler with fewer investment choices. In contrast, products or funds you join through an intermediary usually offer lots of investment and insurance choices, which reinforces why their fees are higher.

Conversely, this means if you want extra features like bundled support from a financial adviser or lots of investment choices, you should expect to pay higher fees.

It works the other way, too. Some super funds or products charge quite high fees even though what they are offering is very simple.

Is not-for-profit better?

Industry funds often describe themselves asnot-for-profit, meaning their fees generally match their costs because they do not need to make a profit for any shareholders. Retail funds, i.e., master trusts, on the other hand, because they are operated by commercial entities must try to make a profit and so they have to charge fees that are more than their costs.

But while being not-for-profit sounds noble, the hard-nosed question is whether being not-for-profit makes a fund better, or does it just make it different?

At *Money* we take a more nuanced view. This is because you should always compare funds' investment returns, choices, fees, insurance and extra features. Being not-for-profit doesn't make the fund bette; it just explains its background and where it came from.

You are now ready to work through *The Good Super Guide* fund comparison table.

Fees rule of thumb

If your super fund or product is charging more than 1% per annum in fees, then it should be providing lots of choices, adviser support, great online account access and extra services. If it isn't, then you should ask it why.

Feature to look for	Fund score
Who runs the fund or product	
Is it clear who runs the fund or product?	Yes / No
Name the company or sponsoring entity	
Do I recognise them and their brand?	Yes / No
Joining	
Can I join online?	Yes / No
How do I rate the online account access?	Good / Okay / Poor
Investments	
How many investment choices does it offer?	
Do I understand how my money will be invested?	Yes / No
How good is the flagship investment choice over 5 years?	
Can I choose investment strategies?	Yes / No
Can I choose to invest in specific asset classes?	Yes / No
Can I choose specific investment managers?	Yes / No
Are underlying shareholdings disclosed?	Yes / No
Can I choose indexed investments?	Yes / No
Can I invest in an ethical or ESG choices?	Yes / No
Can I choose an age-based (lifestage) strategy?	Yes / No
Can I choose my own direct investments?	Yes / No
Insurance	
How much insurance cover do I get as standard?	
How much will death and TPD insurance cost?	$ per week
How much will income protection cost?	$ per week
Can I top-up my insurance?	Yes / No
If I don't want insurance, can I turn it off?	Yes / No
Fees	
How much will I pay in total fees?	% pa
Extras	
Does it come with the support of a financial adviser?	Yes / No
What loyalty discounts are included?	
Can I get discounted health insurance?	Yes / No
Does it have a smartphone or tablet app?	Yes / No
Is there a good range of other extra features?	Yes / No

Super for small business owners

Superannuation has been designed for employees, not for business owners. But with the right advice, small business owners can use their business assets to boost their superannuation.

Entity refers to an individual, partnership, company or trust.

A **CGT concession stakeholder** is either a significant individual in the company or trust and also a spouse of the individual, who participates in the voting, receipt of dividends, income or capital distributions.

Building a business can take time and money. Did you know that for assets held by a small business, if sold, the proceeds can be contributed into super to increase your retirement savings significantly?

It is hard work being self-employed, and probably the last thing you'll be thinking about is your own superannuation. You've got overheads, mortgage repayments, salaries and insurance, and you need to keep the business running.

There are four capital gains tax (CGT) concessions for small business regarding the sale of a CGT asset (see the table on the next page). If sold, the proceeds of the sale of CGT assets used in a small business can be contributed into superannuation. However, there are certain conditions that must be satisfied before these concessions can be applied.

Following below is a general summary that describes how these CGT business concessions work. But it's a complex area that usually requires some consultation with an accountant or tax adviser.

Basic conditions

Certain basic conditions must be met by the small business for it to be eligible for the small business CGT tax concessions, such as:

- net value of the assets owned must not exceed $6 million or the aggregated turnover of the entity and related entities must be less than $2 million.
- active asset test – the asset sold was used or held by the small business for explicit use in a business.
- additional conditions apply to an asset being sold as a share in a company or interest in a trust:
- the entity claiming the concession must be a CGT concession stakeholder in the company or trust. If there is an interposed entity between the CGT concession stakeholder and the company or trust in which the shares or interests are held, the stakeholder must have at least 90% participation.

Small business CGT concessions

There are four small business CGT concessions available to a business owner for the sale of a CGT asset, as shown in the following table.

CGT concessions	Summary
15-year exemption	Probably the most favourable of all the concessions. The entire capital gain can be disregarded and capital losses are not offset against the gain. The asset must have been owned for 15 years before the sale.
Small business 50% active	A small business may qualify for the 50% active asset reduction to its capital gain. Also, if the asset is owned by an individual or trust, the 50% CGT discount can also be applied.
Small business retirement exemption	This exemption allows an entity to disregard a capital gain up to $500,000. This amount can be contributed into super if you are under age 55.
Small business rollover relief	This concession basically defers the capital gain on the sale of an asset where the asset is being replaced or expanded to improve an existing asset.

The amount you can contribute into superannuation comes at a lifetime cap of $1.615 million for the 2021/22 financial year (the cap is indexed), which means the proceeds of the sale of an asset can count towards the lifetime cap and not affect your non-concessional cap.

The CGT lifetime cap contributions arising from the application of the following two concessions:

- The small business 15-year exemption.
- The small business retirement exemption.

KEY POINTS

- Small business owners need to understand the capital gains tax (CGT) lifetime cap and how the CGT concessions work.

- But they should talk to their tax accountant because these arrangements can be complex.

Sharon, age 64, has owned her cattle farm since 2000 and sells it in 2021. By disposing of the farm and assuming that a capital gain was triggered, Sharon could apply the 15-year exemption to disregard the capital gain.

Sharon received $950,000 from the proceeds of the sale of the farm and she's eligible to contribute to superannuation. Sharon can make a CGT lifetime cap contribution of up to $950,000 (the proceeds of the sale).

Case study

David's company has applied the small business retirement exemption and has made a respective payment of $300,000 to David.

David is age 53 and wishes to contribute these monies to superannuation. David has some options available to him, which include:

- making a non-concessional contribution of $300,000 invoking the bring-forward rule
- making a non-concessional contribution of $100,000 and a CGT lifetime cap contribution of $200,000
- making a CGT lifetime cap contribution of $300,000.

David needs to consider the possibility of further non-concessional contributions in the same year or a future financial year when he makes a decision.

Contributions relating to the 15-year exemption

If a business owner applies the small business 15-year exemption (the asset was owned for at least 15 years) towards their assessable capital gain, the proceeds can be contributed to superannuation as a CGT lifetime cap. There are other conditions that must be met, but this gives you a basic understanding of the exemption.

Contributions relating to the retirement exemption

If you apply the small business retirement exemption, a capital gain can be exempted to an amount of

$500,000 (this amount is not indexed), and the exempt amount can be contributed to superannuation as a CGT lifetime cap contribution.

Tip: If you are age 55 or younger, the retirement exemption amount must be contributed in superannuation; if you are over age 55, there is no requirement to direct the amount into superannuation.

The small business CGT concessions are a strategy that can save you a lot of tax, and can also boost your superannuation savings.

The small business CGT concessions are generally considered in the following order:

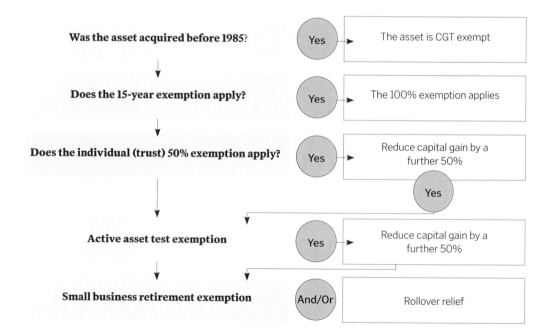

Super choice checklist

Looking for a MySuper product or super fund you can rely on? This checklist should help you.

Fund quality and administration

- Does the fund have a **AAA Quality Assessment Rating**?

- Do you understand how the super fund(s) work and what makes them special? Test yourself by explaining how they work to a friend.

- Who runs the fund, i.e., who is behind it? Have you heard of them? What are their credentials? Do you trust they'll be around for a long time? Who do you call if something goes wrong?

- Have you road tested the fund? Are its **annual member statements** easy to understand? Do the fund information booklets contain all the information you need?

ESG

- If sustainable and ethical investments are important to you, does your fund follow sustainable and ethical investment principles? Does it disclose what it invests in, its diversity practices, support climate change action, declared its position on modern slavery or offer an ESG investment choice? Are you convinced it's genuinely committed to these principles and practices and can prove it?

Investment options and performance

- Do you understand the fund's investment menus?

- How do the **investment returns** stack-up against other funds? Are the investment choices you intend using performing above average, i.e., what is their record over the past three, five or even 10 years?

Fees

- What TOTAL fees will you pay each year, and what do you get for this? For example, average fund fees are now around 1% but the sharpest priced funds charge less than 0.7%. If you are paying more, what are you getting that's special?

Insurance

- Does the fund offer insurance and what types, i.e., death only, death and TPD, income protection? What does it cost? Do you trust the fund will look after you if you need to claim?

- If you are thinking of changing MySuper products or funds, is the new insurance deal better than the deal you already have and will you be automatically accepted for cover in the new fund?

Additional benefits and services

- Does the fund have a reasonable range of extra features that you will actually use? e.g., does it have online account access, webchat, an app, is the website good enough, does it offer deals on health insurance?

Remember that if you have super in more than one MySuper product or super fund, maybe you should also think about consolidating them into your favourite fund. Every smart super fund will help you do this. If you want extra advice and you want to consult a professional financial adviser near you, please visit our sister service SelectAdviser: selectadviser.com.au.

MySuper products directory

MySuper product name	Fund offering the product	Product Unique Identifier	Rating
Active Super Accumulation Scheme	Local Government Super	28901371321258	AAA
ADF Super	Commonwealth Superannuation Corporation	90302247344958	AAA
AMG Corporate Super	AMG Super	30099320583624	AAA
AMIST Super Employer	Australian Meat Industry Superannuation Trust	28342064803589	AAA
AMP SignatureSuper	AMP Superannuation Savings Trust	78421957449538	
ANZ Smart Choice Super - Employer	Retirement Portfolio Service	61808189263840	AAA
ANZ Staff Super - Employee	ANZ Australian Staff Superannuation Scheme	83810127567770	AAA
Asgard Employee Super	Asgard Independence Plan Division Two	90194410365092	
Australia Post Super - Member Savings	Australia Post Superannuation Scheme	42045077895987	
Australian Catholic - Employer	Australian Catholic Superannuation and Retirement Fund	24680629023451	AAA
Australian Ethical Super	Australian Ethical Retail Superannuation Fund	49633667743656	AAA
AustralianSuper	AustralianSuper	65714394898856	AAA
AvSuper Corporate	AvSuper Fund	84421446069940	AAA
Aware Super - Employer Sponsored	Aware Super	53226460365073	AAA
Bendigo SmartStart - Employer	The Bendigo Superannuation Plan	57526653420532	AAA
BOC Gases Super	BOC Gases Superannuation Fund	49620344668116	
BT Business Super	Westpac Mastertrust - Superannuation Division	81236903448174	
BT MySuper	Retirement Wrap	39827542991267	AAA
BUSSQ MySuper	Building Unions Superannuation Scheme (Queensland)	85571332201413	AAA
CareSuper	Care Super	98172275725867	AAA
Catholic Super	MyLifeMyMoney Superannuation Fund	50237896957714	AAA
CBA Group Super - Accumulate Plus	Commonwealth Bank Group Super	24248426878648	AAA
Cbus Industry Super	Construction and Building Unions Superannuation Fund	75493363262473	AAA
CFS - FirstChoice Employer Super	Colonial First State FirstChoice Superannuation Trust	26458298557923	AAA
Christian Super	Christian Super	66628776348908	AAA
Club Plus Industry Division	Club Plus Superannuation Scheme	95275115088045	AAA
EISS Super	Energy Industries Superannuation Scheme - Pool A	22277243559311	AAA
Energy Super	Energy Super	33761363685380	AAA
Equip MyFuture	Equipsuper	33813823017672	AAA
Essential Super - Employer	Commonwealth Essential Super	56601925435909	
First Super - Employer Sponsored	First Super	56286625181006	AAA
GS & JB Were Super Fund	Goldman Sachs & JBWere Superannuation Fund	55697537183245	
GuildSuper	Guild Retirement Fund	22599554834526	AAA
HESTA	Health Employees Superannuation Trust Australia	64971749321585	AAA
Hostplus	Hostplus Superannuation Fund	68657495890198	AAA
Intrust Super - Core Super	Hostplus Superannuation Fund	65704511371601	AAA

MySuper product name	Fund offering the product	Product Unique Identifier	Rating
IOOF Employer Super - Employer	IOOF Portfolio Service Superannuation Fund	70815369818036	AAA
IPE - Super	Incitec Pivot Employees Superannuation Fund	68569795856660	
legalsuper	legalsuper	60346078879190	AAA
LESF and Macmahon Super	OneSuper	43905581638357	
LGIAsuper Accumulation	LGIAsuper	23053121564638	AAA
LUCRF Super	Labour Union Co-operative Retirement Fund	26382680883067	AAA
Lutheran Super	Lutheran Super	93371348387621	AAA
Maritime Super	Maritime Super	77455663441220	AAA
Media Super	Media Super	42574421650098	AAA
Mercer Super Trust - Corporate	Mercer Super Trust	19905422981252	AAA
Mercy Super	Mercy Super	11789425178832	AAA
MIESF	Meat Industry Employees Superannuation Fund	17317520544110	
MLC MasterKey Business Super	MLC Super Fund	70732426024883	
NGS Super Accumulation	NGS Super	73549180515789	AAA
Prime Super	Prime Super	60562335823668	AAA
PSS accumulation plan	Commonwealth Superannuation Corporation	65127917725842	AAA
Qantas Super Gateway	Qantas Superannuation Plan	41272198829376	AAA
QSuper Accumulation Account	QSuper	6.09051E+13	AAA
REI Super	REI Super	7.66417E+13	AAA
Rest Super	Retail Employees Superannuation Trust	6.26537E+13	AAA
Russell iQ Super Employer	Russell Investments Master Trust	8.93848E+13	
smartMonday PRIME	Aon Master Trust	6.89647E+13	AAA
Spirit Super	Spirit Super	7.45594E+13	AAA
StatewideSuper	Statewide Superannuation Trust	5.41452E+13	AAA
Suncorp Brighter Super for business	Suncorp Master Trust	9.8351E+13	
Sunsuper for Life Business	Sunsuper Superannuation Fund	9.85031E+13	AAA
TASPLAN	Spirit Super	1.4602E+13	AAA
Telstra Super Corporate Plus	Telstra Superannuation Scheme	8.55021E+13	AAA
Toyota Super	Toyota Super	5.82084E+13	
TWUSUPER	TWU Superannuation Fund	7.73436E+13	AAA
UniSuper	Unisuper	9.13859E+13	AAA
VicSuper FutureSaver	Aware Super	5.32265E+13	AAA
Virgin Money Super Employer	Mercer Super Trust	1.99054E+13	AAA
Vision Super Saver	Local Authorities Superannuation Fund	2.44966E+13	AAA
VISSF Accumulation	Victorian Independent Schools Super Fund	3.70249E+13	AAA
WA Super Super Solutions - Employer	Aware Super	1.81595E+13	AAA

* Formerly known as First State Super

Retirement income streams

When you retire you need to ensure you will get regular income. One way to do this is by choosing the right retirement income stream product. But what are they and how do you choose between them?

KEY POINTS

- Retirement income stream products are special financial products designed to pay retirees a regular income. Some have facilities to help manage your investments.

- When you retire you should consult with Centrelink, your super fund and a financial adviser.

- Different types of retirement income steam products are designed with different features. This can make choosing between them complex.

- After you've retired you won't pay annual income tax on earnings on at least the first $1.6 million and potentially up to $1.7 million of your superannuation savings. But earnings from the rest are taxed at 15%.

You've worked hard for years and saved up a sizeable nest egg and now you want to retire. This simple decision, however, puts you right into the thick of having to make up your mind about how to structure your retirement income so you can maximise your Centrelink entitlements while also minimising your tax liabilities and ensuring that your money lasts as long as possible.

The type of financial products you use to structure your retirement income this way are known as a retirement income streams. These are products specially designed to pay you regular income, with some products also enabling you to manage your investments. These features make these products more complex than normal pre-retirement superannuation funds.

To make this decision process as smooth as it can be, when you retire or are approaching retirement, you should:

1. Contact Centrelink and arrange to speak to one of its financial information services officers. These specialists are not financial advisers but they will explain to you what your Centrelink entitlements are, how the assets and income tests work, what retirement income stream options you might have and how you might wish to structure things to maximise your entitlements regarding the age pension, healthcare and other ancillary benefits.
2. Talk to your superannuation fund, because it probably already has a range of specially designed retirement income stream products, and you should try to understand how they work and which ones might be suitable for you.
3. Arrange a meeting with your financial adviser, if you have one, because choosing the right retirement income stream product is complex. If you don't have your own independent adviser, make an appointment to speak to one associated with your superannuation fund.

As you work through these steps you will start to understand the interlocking taxation, superannuation, investment, social security, psychological and personal issues that must be resolved before you can confidently choose your retirement income stream product.

What are your income needs?

The Association of Superannuation Funds of Australia (ASFA) estimates, based on its regular Retirement Standard surveys of retirees, that for a "comfortable" retirement lifestyle you will need $63,352 p.a. if you are in a couple relationship or $44,818 p.a. if you are a single person. For a "modest" retirement lifestyle, ASFA says you will need $41,170 p.a. and $28,514 p.a. respectively.

The amount of income you need each year will vary depending on your lifestyle expectations, expenses, where you live, your family situation, your life expectancy and health. But regardless of whether you think you need to prepare for a comfortable or modest standard of living in retirement, a good way to think about your retirement is to separate it into at least two core elements:

- Basic necessary income to meet all daily expenses, e.g., housing, food, utilities, clothes etc.

Fun fact:
Two-thirds of older Australians rely on the government age pension or a related allowance as their main source of personal income in retirement.

Explainer – transfer balance cap

On July 1, 2017, the government introduced the concept of the transfer balance cap (TBC). which is the maximum amount you can transfer from your regular superannuation account, which is taxed at a nominal rate of 15%, into a retirement account, which is tax-free. Any residual is left in your regular superannuation account, meaning its earnings are taxed at the standard 15% rate.

For 2021/22, the general TBC is $1.7 million. This cap will apply to you if you have not yet commenced a retirement income stream.

However, if you commenced a retirement income stream prior to July 1, 2021, then your personal TBC will be set between $1.6 million and $1.7 million. You should consult a financial adviser to assist you with calculating the maximum amount of your tax-free retirement savings.

- Discretionary income to cover irregular expenses, e.g., holidays, entertainment, healthcare etc.

You need a greater level of certainty to meet your daily income needs, meaning it should be regular and preferably stable income. Discretionary income, on the other hand, enables you to maintain your desired lifestyle and meet unexpected expenses. This income can be generated from your regular income source or through withdrawals from your retirement income account, i.e., by accessing your capital.

Once your income needs are met, you should put aside some cash as a reserve. Any money that is left over can be invested in growth assets to build capital for future needs or to help provide a growing income stream to increase your discretionary income lifestyle component.

Another issue to be aware of is that when you retire you may become risk-averse, i.e., more fearful of investment risks than you were before you retired. This is because you may believe you won't have time nor opportunity to replace any capital losses if the market suffers a downturn. But take note, when most people retire, they should be planning for a 20-year-plus time frame. For their savings to last over this period, they need some growth assets in their portfolio to at least deal with inflation. It is also important to consider that your total income needs may not reduce as you age, even though the components of what income you need might.

Handling your longevity risk
Australia has the third-highest life expectancy of any country in the world and it is not unreasonable for retirees to expect to live beyond 85 years of age. If you are healthy, highly educated or have been earning a reasonable income throughout your working life, chances are you will live longer still. This has a big impact on your retirement income planning.

The age pension payment retirees receive will also most likely be less than what many people need to live on, at least according to ASFA. As a result, most retirees can't afford for their private superannuation investments to run out. If this happens, it could severely affect their standard of living in their older years.

Adding even more complexity, the age at which the age pension can be accessed is also increasing just as the asset test thresholds are decreasing – so you may need more savings to be self-sufficient than you planned, particularly in the earlier years of your retirement. Illustrating this, on July 1, 2021, it increased to 66 years and six months if you were born from July 1, 1955 to December 31, 1956, inclusive. This age threshold is gradually increasing and by 2023 it will be 67 years if you were born on or after January 1, 1957.

Social security and your retirement
Social security benefits, being the age pension and other entitlements, are available to retirees to top up their private income, provided they satisfy the eligibility criteria. This system aims to ensure that everyone is able to at least purchase the basic necessities of life. Veterans receive their payments through the Department of Veterans' Affairs (DVA).

These payments and their amount are based on your age, relationship status, and assets and income levels.

The maximum age pension is indexed each six months in March and September. This indexation is generally linked to the consumer price index (CPI). The age pension for a single person is guaranteed to remain at least equal to 27.7% of the male total average weekly earnings (MTAWE). For couples it is guaranteed to be at least equal 67%.

Account- vs non-account based income streams

Account-based income streams place the individual in charge of their retirement account in much the same way that most individuals are in charge of their superannuation accumulation account during their working lives. Account-based income streams are the most popular type of income stream for Australians who convert their accumulated superannuation into an income stream. Reflecting this, account-based income streams can only be purchased with superannuation money.

Non-account-based income streams involve contracting with either a superannuation fund or a life insurance company to provide an income stream. They are generally for a fixed term or your lifetime:

- **Fixed-term**. Paid over a specific term at a rate that is fixed according to your life expectancy and the amount of capital deposited into it at commencement.
- **Lifetime**. These income streams last as long as you do. As with the fixed term, the income level is pre-agreed. However, unlike other income streams, the income from lifetime income streams is guaranteed for your lifetime, no matter what happens to you or the investment markets.

You don't have to choose one or the other because they can work together. Non-account-based income streams may be used to provide your basic income needs (i.e., to reduce uncertainty) and you can combine this with an account-based pension for your discretionary income needs or to produce higher potential returns to help manage inflation risk. Account-based pensions are, however, used by most retirees to fund all or most of their income needs because they provide greater flexibility in both timing and amounts that can be withdrawn.

But there's a new breed of account-based pension emerging that guarantee to pay a certain amount of income for life, even after the account balance reduces to nil. These are often generically referred to as longevity income streams or deferred income streams, but they can operate under various other marketing names.

The table on the next page summarises the features generally offered by the different types of income stream types. It will help you decide which type is best for you.

Account-based minimum drawdowns

If you have an account-based retirement income stream, you are required to take a minimum payment from it each year. This is because it's a retirement product, and the government wants to encourage you to spend the money on yourself rather than leave it all in your estate.

Using the money in your account-based pension also makes you less reliant on the age pension, which is the whole reason why we have superannuation in the first place.

The minimum payment is calculated using specified percentage factors based on your age. No maximum income limit applies unless it is a transition-to-retirement (TTR) income stream, where the maximum is 10% of the account balance at the start of each financial year. The minimum drawdown rates have been reduced by the government (for 2020/21 and 2021/22) in response to the COVID-19 pandemic.

Fees

The types of fees you are likely to pay your income stream provider will vary depending on the provider

Minimum drawdowns applying in 2020/21

Age of beneficiary	Previous annual percentage factor	2020/21 annual percentage factor
Under 65	4%	2%
65-74	5%	2.5%
75-79	6%	3%
80-84	7%	3.5%
85-89	9%	4.5%
90-94	11%	5.5%
95 or older	14%	7%

and how many and what types of features it has. As with super during the accumulation phase, the main types of fees are ongoing management fees, member fees and investment fees. But because you now receive regular income, there will often be a regular extra administration fee associated with your provider having to make these payments. According to Rainmaker Information's latest 2021 retirement income stream fee survey, these products cost on average 1.1% p.a.

Other factors likely to increase your fees are that the more investment choices available in your income stream product the more expensive it can be. The investments you choose for your portfolio, especially in account-based pensions, and how often you wish to receive regular payments can also affect your fees. For example, you should expect to pay higher fees if you wish to receive 12 monthly payments rather than just one annual payment.

Types of retirement income streams

| Common product name | Account-based | Non-account-based | | |
	Allocated	Lifetime	Fixed term	Life expectancy
For people who want low risk	✗	✓	✓	✓
Guaranteed level of regular payments	✗	✓	✓	✓
Can vary payments to suit requirements	✓	✗	✗	✗
Can draw down extra capital	✓	✗	✗	✗
Can choose investments	✓	✗	✗	✗
Can transfer residual capital value to estate	✓	✗	✗	✗
Preferred beneficiary can get reversionary payment	✓	✓	✓	✓

Adapted by Rainmaker Information from Department of Human Services.

Transition to retirement pension

If you've reached preservation age (i.e., the age at which you can begin accessing your superannuation benefits) and are still working, a transition-to-retirement (TTR) pension may suit you. TTRs can be used in conjunction with increased concessional contributions to reduce your working hours while maintaining your income or to reduce your tax. Many super funds that offer account-based income streams also offer TTR pensions. An important feature of TTR pensions is that they do not count towards your lifetime transfer balance cap. Before signing up to a TTR you should get financial advice.

Self-managed super user guide

So far in *The Good Super Guide* we have talked about how super choice will affect you and how you can go about choosing a superannuation fund. But what if you want to manage your superannuation yourself in your own self-managed super fund?

KEY POINTS

- Most people use super funds operated by someone else, but you can do it yourself by setting up a self-managed superannuation fund (SMSF).

- Running your own SMSF is much more complex that being a member of a regular super fund.

- SMSFs have a range of special rules and requirements. You can handle these yourself, or you can work with a financial adviser, accountant or specialist SMSF administrator.

- Your SMSF is just a structure for how you want to organise your superannuation. You still have to get the investments working properly to achieve good investment returns.

In examining all the types of superannuation funds available, we have talked about workplace and personal super funds, and we have also talked about public offer superannuation funds (funds that are open to the public). In all these types of funds, we have been referring to funds that are run by someone else.

But what if you want to manage your superannuation yourself? If you do this it means you take on responsibility for the fund as you become the fund trustee, and you have to arrange its administration, fulfil compliance obligations, and organise its investments. You can also nominate your SMSF to become your preferred choice fund to receive your employer-paid contributions.

You can arrange for other people to look after these tasks for you, but when you run the fund, the buck stops with you. After all, that's why these are called self-managed superannuation funds.

SMSFs – things to consider
SMSFs can't invest in just anything
Running your own SMSF doesn't mean you can do anything you want with the investments. When you run an SMSF, you are a trustee and you are responsible for everything the fund does. To make sure SMSFs are run properly, the government has created a range of special rules for SMSFs to make sure the money in them is used and invested properly and that the funds themselves are operated appropriately.

If you think that running your own SMSF means you can bend the investment rules, e.g., to use your superannuation to buy your house or your business, don't start an SMSF.

An SMSF is just a structure

You don't invest in an SMSF but, rather, use it as a way to structure or organise your superannuation. In this way they are an alternative to funds administered by arm's length trustees. The main advantages of SMSFs are that members, who are also required to be trustees, have greater control and flexibility over investment decisions and so can tailor the overall operation of the fund to suit their needs. There are also some taxation advantages compared to other types of funds due to the timing of investments and possible cost advantages. But all the normal superannuation tax rules still apply.

You'll need around $250,000

If you have enough money in super, running your own SMSF can be surprisingly cost effective. But even though their cost ratios can be among the lowest of all fund types, in dollar terms, they can still cost several thousand dollars each year to run when you take into account their initial set-up costs, ongoing administration and compliance costs, and the investment transaction and management fees.

As a result, many SMSF experts use the rule of

!

Consumer warning:
If you want simple, easy superannuation do NOT set up your own SMSF. This is because when you have an SMSF you are in the business of running a superannuation fund, and the rules you have to follow are much more complex than if you are a member of a typical super fund.

thumb that for an SMSF to be cost effective it needs at least $250,000. This threshold is based on the finding that the average SMSF costs about $2,500 annually and this converts to a total expense ratio (TER) of 1%, which is about the same TER as many MySuper products.

Adding more subtlety, many SMSFs below $1 million don't achieve the same investment performance as the average MySuper product. So while the flexibility available in an SMSF is very attractive, trustees should manage them with the clear objective to achieve strong investment returns.

What it costs to run an SMSF

It costs an average of $2,500 each year to run an SMSF. For an SMSF with about $250,000 in assets this converts to a TER of about 1%. The fee ratio, however, can be much higher for small SMSFs but much lower for large SMSFs. There are three main types of costs for SMSFs:

1. **Set-up costs** that average about $600 but can range up to more than $1,000.
2. **Ongoing administration and compliance costs** that average about $1,200 but can range up to more than $5,000.
3. **Investment costs**, which vary depending on how complex the SMSF's investment portfolio is and how often it transacts, i.e., buys a new investment, sells shares, deposits money into a term deposit, acquires a property. The guide is that the investment costs should average around 0.5% p.a., which for a $250,000 portfolio is around $1,250.

These combined costs mean that in your SMSF's first year, the fund may cost $3,000, or about 1.2% of your portfolio (assuming assets of $250,000). However, as most of the fees, apart from the investment fee, are usually fixed costs, as the SMSF gets larger these costs as a ratio of the overall portfolio should reduce. SMSFs above $1 million can have cost ratios well below 1%, which makes them very attractive for fund members with large superannuation balances.

SMSF trust deeds must include:

- The proper name of the fund.
- Names of the fund trustees, how they are appointed, and how and on what basis they can be removed from being a trustee of the fund.
- Details of the corporate trustee the fund will appoint to manage its affairs (if you choose to have one).
- A statement that the fund is established for the sole purpose of providing old-age and retirement benefits to the fund members. (Refer also to the section on SMSF investment rules for more details about the sole-purpose test rule.)
- A statement that the fund trustees will not accept any payments to carry out their roles with the fund.
- Details of how members' benefits will be calculated and paid.
- Details of what contribution types the fund will accept.
- Details of who can become a member of the fund.
- Rules for how the fund will be wound up if the need arises.

Creating a trust deed for your SMSF

Your SMSF must have its own trust deed, which is a list of rules for how the fund operates, deals with its members, pays benefits, and handles its investments.

This trust deed is required for the simple reason that superannuation in Australia is based upon Trust Law, and under this law you must always have a set of predetermined and agreed rules in place so everyone associated with the fund knows what to expect. In case of any disputes, it will be this trust deed that will be used as the basis for determining if the fund was properly managed.

Standard form templated trust deeds can be obtained from special SMSF advisers, so finding one isn't difficult. But equally you should make sure your trust deed is properly set up as it will be very expensive to fix things later if something isn't right.

Individual or corporate trustees

After you have established or obtained your SMSF's trust deed, you then need to appoint its trustees and decide if they should be individuals or a corporate trustee. Having individual trustees can be simpler and comes with lower compliance costs/burden, but if something goes wrong the individual trustees could be liable. Using corporate trustees, however, means the liability is held by the trustee company. It's also much simpler for succession planning, i.e., when members exit or new ones join the fund.

The rules SMSFs should follow when appointing their trustees include:

- If appointing a corporate trustee, establish rules governing how that company will operate and who will be its directors.

- If appointing individual trustees, each trustee must also be a member of the fund.
- No member of the fund can be employed by any other member, unless they are family members.
- There must be no more than six members in the fund.
- Trustees cannot be paid to carry out their trustee roles.

If these rules are met, you need to apply to the ATO to formally set up your SMSF (part of which means "electing" to be regulated by the ATO). You must then arrange a tax file number (TFN) and establish a bank account for the SMSF (the bank account is so you can keep the SMSF's money and transactions of the super fund separate to those of the trustees as individuals). It may also help for the SMSF to have an Australian business number (ABN), though this isn't compulsory.

What super contributions will your SMSF accept?

Your SMSF trust deed must state what types of super payments it will accept. For example, will it accept contributions from each member's employer? Will it accept rollovers from other super funds? Will it accept contributions from each member's non-working spouse (so-called spouse accounts)? Will it accept contributions from and for children, and if so under what conditions?

While it would be easiest for your SMSF to simply say it will accept all types of super contributions, the nature of super is that the rules for an SMSF have to be more specific because there is no one-size-fits-all definition of what the term "super contribution" actually means.

Reinforcing these rules around super contributions, SMSFs cannot accept non-cash contributions from related parties and cannot allow assets belonging to members to be transferred into the fund unless they satisfy special provisions in the general superannuation rules. For example, they must not make up more than 5% of the fund's assets, they must be listed securities assets (such as shares, bonds, or units in a managed fund), or they are real business property. See the later section in this chapter on SMSF investment rules.

Setting up your investment objectives and strategies

As part of setting up an SMSF, trustees must develop and officially record clear investment objectives and strategies to support their objective. For example, if the SMSF has members close to retirement age, some or all of the investment objectives and strategies of the fund might be more conservative.

Examples of questions your investment strategy may cover include:

- What types of assets will your SMSF invest in?

What if you don't want to be a trustee?

While some people like the idea of running their own fund, not everyone wants to be the trustee. Further, some people are not allowed to be SMSF trustees because they may be undischarged bankrupts or have engaged in other activities that make them a disqualified person.

This, however, shouldn't cause any problems if you are willing to appoint an Approved Trustee to your SMSF to act as the trustee. SMSFs that operate this way are known as Small APRA Funds (SAFs). Because you are paying someone else to be trustee, they are more expensive to operate than normal SMSFs.

Despite these differences in how the trustees operate, these SAFs have all the same investment, compliance and administration rules that apply to regular SMSFs.

For example: domestic or overseas shares, bonds, listed or direct property, residential or commercial property, derivatives, managed funds, cash deposits, collectables..

- What proportion, or range of proportions, of its investments will it place into each asset class? For example: between nil and 55% in shares, between nil and 25% in cash, and nil and 40% in property.
- How will the investment decisions of the SMSF be made? For example: by a vote of the trustees; with the advice of a financial adviser or a stockbroker.
- How often will the fund's investments be reviewed, and how will this review be conducted? For example: will the SMSF's investments be reviewed each year, each quarter, each month? And who will conduct the review?
- How should the investments be assessed and measured? For example: by comparison against a benchmark, and if so what benchmark?
- Have the insurance needs of members been considered? For example: do they already have insurance outside super? Are they underinsured?
- Did the member decline to take out any insurance?

Your investment strategy is not restricted to these issues, but if it covers most, if not all, of them, then it will be a very robust strategy that should easily pass muster. You are also required to document the strategy and to keep minutes of meetings held by the trustees to discuss the investments of the fund. These minutes must be kept for at least 10 years.

Investment restrictions

An SMSF must be maintained solely for the purpose of providing retirement benefits to members or to their dependants, if the member dies. Breaching the sole-purpose test can lead to the trustee facing both criminal and civil penalties. Penalties can include up to five years' imprisonment and a fine up

The Good Super Guide SMSF checklist

After setting up your SMSF's trust deed, appointing the trustees, preparing the investment strategy document and deciding upon the investments, the next step is to make sure your SMSF satisfies all the annual administration and compliance rules. These include:

- lodging annual taxation and superannuation returns with the various regulators
- lodging member contribution statements
- reporting all member benefit payments
- appointing auditors to complete the annual audit review
- establishing a system to maintain the fund's records (which must be kept for at least 10 years)
- ensuring that the SMSF has not violated any of the investment rules.

These administration tasks can be handled yourself or you can outsource them to an accountant, financial adviser or SMSF specialist administrator, noting that some records have to be kept for at least five years: for example, accounting records that explain the transactions and financial position of the fund, annual operating statements, annual statements of the fund's financial position, and copies of all annual returns that were lodged.

Records that have to be kept for at least 10 years include minutes of trustee meetings where fund business was discussed, details about changes of trustees and members' written consent to be appointed as trustees, and copies of all reports given to members.

How popular are SMSFs?

As at March 2021, there were 597,396 SMSFs run by just under 1.121 million Australians. The number of SMSFs in previous years used to grow by about 20,000 each year but has recently slowed. These funds hold just 8% of all superannuation accounts but almost one-third of all superannuation savings. SMSFs have the lowest fees of any superannuation market segment, averaging about 0.35% for administration and compliance before adding investment costs.

to 2,000 penalty points, with each point currently worth $222. A breach of the sole-purpose test is also likely to result in the fund being deemed non-complying, in which case, both current and past tax concessions can be reversed, leading to a significant tax bill.

It can be very tempting for the trustees of an SMSF to invest in assets that provide current benefits to members, but in doing so you are jeopardising your compliance with the sole-purpose test. It is important to note, however, that the regulator, in this case the ATO, is concerned with the purpose of the investment, not the type of investment, e.g., an SMSF might invest in some quite exotic investments and still comply with the sole-purpose test.

Trustees are permitted only to acquire assets from a "related party" of the fund where the acquisition of the asset will NOT result in the "in-house" assets of the fund exceeding 5% of all assets. Related parties include members, trustees and employers who contribute to the fund. Related parties also include relatives of members. SMSFs are, however, allowed to acquire business real property from related parties which exceeds 5% of all assets.

Superannuation funds are not allowed to borrow longer-term monies in order to gear up returns. SMSFs can, however, use a separate trust to undertake leveraged investments. Trustees are not allowed to lend money or provide financial assistance to members or related parties.

All transactions must be made on an arm's length basis, that is, on strictly commercial terms. The purchase and sale price of an asset should always reflect the true market value. Income from assets should always reflect the true market rate of return.

The relationship between trustees and members in SMSFs means that members are in a position where they may try to push the investment restriction boundaries – sometimes beyond what

the auditors and regulators deem acceptable. While members of large superannuation funds might be also tempted to breach the investment rules, in reality the separation between trustee and member in large funds is such that members are not really in a position to breach the rules.

Collectibles and artworks

SMSFs may invest in collectables, e.g., artworks, but the investments must be independently valued and appropriately authenticated. The SMSF must also insure the artworks in the name of the fund and store them according to the conditions of the insurer – a condition of ownership that can nullify the reasons some SMSFs want to own these types of assets. Trustees must also be able to reasonably demonstrate the commercial value of any lease or exhibition terms and conditions.

Tax and other useful facts

These pages contain general information about tax rates and thresholds for super contributions and benefits.

The main thing to understand about how super is taxed is that it used to be taxed at three points – on the way in as contributions, inside the fund as earnings and on the way out as benefits. However, for most people past the age of 60, super is now effectively tax-free. If you have more than $1.6 million in superannuation the portion above this threshold will be taxed but only at 15%. But regardless of how and at what stage superannuation is taxed, it is still taxed at extremely concessional levels compared to other types of investment and this is what makes superannuation so special.

Limits, thresholds and special conditions nonetheless still exist around superannuation tax and it is important that employers, their employees,

consumers and financial advisers properly understand these rules or consult with someone who does.

For example, while an individual or company (on behalf of its employees) may contribute any amount into superannuation, there is a limit to which those contributions attract a tax deduction. Moreover, the government requires all employers to provide a minimum level of superannuation for their employees, called the super guarantee, which is currently equivalent to 10% of an employee's wage or salary.

Some employers may, of course, contribute more and the government has even established a bonus scheme for low-income earners. To find out more about how the government has changed the superannuation taxation rules to make it even more attractive than it was, see ato.gov.au/super. To help you get started, we have prepared the following taxation information tables.

Threshold summary

Financial year	Charge percentage
2014/15 to 2020/21	9.5%
2021/22	10.0%
2022/23	10.5%
2023/24	11.0%
2024/25	11.5%
2025/26 and later years	12.0%

Maximum contribution base	Amount in a quarterly contribution period
2020/21	$57,090
2021/22	$58,920

Superannuation contribution caps	
Concessional 2021/22	$27,500
Concessional 2020/21	$25,000
Total superannuation balance on 30 June, 2021	**Non-concessional (2021/22)**
Under $1.7 million	$110,000
$1.7 million and over	Nil

Eligible termination payment (ETP) threshold	2020/21	2021/22
ETP cap for excluded payments	$215,000	$225,000

Bona fide redundancy payments (tax-free amounts)	2020/21	2021/22
Initial amount	$10,989	$11,341
Additional years	$5,496	$5,672
Company tax rate*	30%	30%

* The full company tax rate of 30% applies to all companies that are not eligible for the lower company tax rate.

Super lump sum tax

Taxed in the fund:

Age	Lump sum	Income stream
Age 60 and over	Tax-free	Tax-free
Preservation age to age 59	0% up to the low rate cap ($225,000 for 2021/22). Amount above $225,000 is subject to tax up to maximum rate of 15% plus Medicare levy	Marginal tax rates and tax offset of 15% of the taxable component.
Below preservation age	Subject to tax up to maximum rate of 20% plus Medicare levy	Marginal tax rates, with no tax offset.

Source: The Australian Taxation Office

Untaxed in the fund:

Age	Lump sum	Income stream
Age 60 and over	Subject to tax up to a maximum of 15% on amount up to the untaxed plan cap amount of $1.615m. Top marginal rates applies to amounts above $1.615m.	Marginal tax rates and tax offset of 10% of element untaxed in the fund.
Preservation age to age 59	Subject to tax up to a maximum of 15% plus Medicare on amount up to the low-rate cap amount of $225,000. Amount exceeding $225,000 up to the untaxed plan cap amount ($1.615m) is taxed at a maximum rate of 30% plus Medicare. Amount exceeding $1.615m is taxed at the top marginal rate.	Marginal tax rates, with no tax offset.
Below preservation age	Amount up to $1.615m is taxed at a maximum rate of 30% plus Medicare. Amount exceeding $1.615m amount is taxed at the top marginal rate.	Taxed at marginal rates, with no tax offset.

Death benefit payments to non-dependants:

Age of deceased	Type of death benefit	Age of recipient	Taxation treatment
Any age	Lump sum	Any age	Element taxed in the fund is taxed at 15%. Element untaxed in the fund is taxed at 30%.
Any age	Income stream	Any age	Cannot be paid as an income stream. Income streams that commenced before July 1, 2007 are taxed as if received by a dependant.

Death benefit payments to dependants:

Age of deceased	Type of death benefit	Age of recipient	Taxation treatment
Any age	Lump sum	Any age	Tax-free (not assessable, not exempt income).
Aged 60 and over	Income stream	Any age	Element taxed in the fund is tax-free. Element untaxed in the fund is taxed at marginal rates with offset of 10% of the element untaxed in the fund.
Below age 60	Income stream	Above age 60	Element taxed in the fund is tax-free. Element untaxed in the fund is taxed at marginal rates with offset of 10% of the element untaxed in the fund.
Below age 60	Income stream	Below age 60	Element taxed in the fund is taxed at marginal rates with offset equal to 15% of the amount. Element untaxed in the fund is taxed at marginal rates.

	Age	Component subject to PAYG withholding	Tax treatment
Superannuation lump sum benefit less than $200	Any	None	Nil
Superannuation lump sum benefit (terminally ill recipient)	Any	None	Nil

Eligible termination payments (ETP) tax

Component	Age when paid	Amount subject to tax	Max tax rate*
Life benefit ETP			
Taxable component	Under preservation age	Up to $225,000	32.00%
	At or above preservation age	Up to $225,000	17.00%
	All ages	Up to $225,000	47.00%
Death benefit ETP paid to non-dependants			
Taxable component	All ages	Up to $225,000	32.00%
		Above $225,000	47.00%
Death benefit ETP paid to dependants			
Taxable component	All ages	Up to $225,000	Nil
		Above $225,000	47.00%
Death benefit ETP paid to dependants			
Taxable component	Taxed in the hands of the beneficiary of the estate, as above, based on whether the beneficiary is a dependant or not.		

* Includes Medicare levy

Super income stream tax

Age of recipient	Element taxed in the fund of a super income stream
Age 60 or above	Tax free
Under 60 but at or above preservation age	Taxed at marginal tax rates, 15% tax offset.
Under preservation age	Taxed at marginal tax rates with no tax offset (15% tax offset available if disability superannuation benefit).

Age of recipient	Element untaxed in the fund of a super income stream
Element untaxed in the fund of a super income stream	Taxed at marginal rates, with a 10% tax offset.
Under 60 but at or above preservation age	Taxed at marginal rates, with no tax offset.
Under preservation age	Taxed at marginal rates, with no tax offset.

Personal marginal income tax rates

Taxable income	Tax
0 - $18,200	Nil
$18,201 - $45,000	$0 +19% >$18,200
$45,001 -$120,00	$5,092 + 32.5% >$45,000
$120,001 - $180,000	$29,467 + 37% >120,000
Over $180,000	$51,667 + 45% >180,000

*The above rates do not include the Medicare levy of 2%

Source: The Australian Taxation Office

Medicare levy surcharge

Family structure				
Singles	Less than $90,000	$90,001-	$105,001-	$140,001 or more
Families (combined)	Less than	$180,001-	$210,001-	$280,001 or more
Medicare levy	0%	1.00%	1.25%	1.50%

* Income thresholds are typically indexed on 1 July with Average weekly ordinary time earnings (AWOTE).

Low income tax offset (LITO)

Lower income threshold	Higher income threshold	Max offset
$0	$37,500	$700
$37,501	$45,000	$700-[(TI - $37,500) x 0.05]
$45,001	$66,666	$325-[(TI - $45,000) x 0.015]
Over $66,667		Nil

Low and middle income tax offset (LMITO)

Lower income threshold	Higher income threshold	Max offset
$0	$37,000	$255
$37,001	$48,000	$255-[(TI - $37,000) x 0.075]
Over $48,001	$90,000	$1,080
$90,001	$126,000	$1,080-[(TI - $90,000) x 0.03]
Over $126,000		Nil

Government co-contributions

Income year	Lower income	Higher income	Max benefit
2021/22	$41,112	$56,112	$500

Low income super tax offset (LISTO)

Amount payable 2020/21	Maximum LISTO contribution	Maximum adjusted taxable income* to be eligible	Income test
15% of concessional contributions up to $3,333	$500	$37,000	10% or more of total income is derived from business or employment

* Adjusted taxable income = taxable income + adjusted fringe benefits total + total foreign income + total net investment loss + tax free pension or benefit + reportable superannuation contributions + less deductible child maintenance expenditure.

Source: The Australian Taxation Office

Age restrictions on contributions

Type of contribution	Under 67	Over 67 but under 75*	75 and over
Super guarantee contributions	Yes	Yes	Yes
Voluntary employer contributions	Yes	Subject to work test	No
Non-concessional contributions	Yes	Subject to work test	No
Spouse contributions	Yes	Subject to work test	No
Government co-contributions	Yes	Yes, if under age 71 at the end of financial year**	No

* Includes on or before 28 days after the end of the month in which the member turns 75 years old.
** To be eligible for the Government co-contribution, you will need to be aged under 74 at the end of financial year.

Minimum drawdowns applying in 2021/22

Age of beneficiary	Previous annual percentage factor	2020/21 annual percentage factor
Under 65	4%	2%
65-74	5%	2.5%
75-79	6%	3%
80-84	7%	3.5%
85-89	9%	4.5%
90-94	11%	5.5%
95 or older	14%	7%

Social security entitlements

Aged pension:

Family situation	Maximum benefit ($ per fortnight)*
Single pensioner	$868.30
Partnered pensioner	$654.40
Couple separated due to ill health (each)	$868.30

As at 1 July 2019 * Pension figures exclude the pension supplement (the maximum pension supplement amount is $69.60 per fortnight for singles and illness-separated couple members; $105 per fortnight combined for couples) and the energy supplement of $14.10 pf for singles and illness-separated couples or $10.60 pf for each member of a couple.

A note about the superannuation fund profiles

The following pages contain profiles of the major providers of superannuation in Australia. These include industry funds, master trusts, implemented consultants, government super funds and self-managed super service providers.

These profiles in themselves do not constitute an offer and they are not a basis for investment. They may help you identify providers for further investigation and help you formulate questions for your consultant or adviser. The profiles are a little like searching for a restaurant online, some pages contain more information than others.

These profiles are grouped into workplace funds, personal funds, self-managed service providers and retirement income providers. Recall that workplace super is arranged through your employer, personal super is a fund you join directly as an individual, and self-managed is when you establish and operate your own super fund.

The super funds that have the enhanced listings are the ones that are supporting you by making this guide possible.

For more information about how these listings were compiled, please call us on 02 8234 7500 or email us at money@moneymag.com.au.

WORKPLACE SUPER PROVIDERS — 93

Workplace super funds are those that are available to employers, whether they are private company or public sector employers. A major feature of these workplace funds is that because they are able to take advantage of the business volume that comes from combining the superannuation buying power of a large number of employees, they often offer wholesale discount fee rates and so are generally cheaper than personal funds.

PERSONAL SUPER PROVIDERS — 115

Personal super funds are those that are available to individual consumers. Because personal super funds are sold to individual consumers rather than to larger scale workplaces, they will usually have to charge fees that are higher than workplace funds. And, because these funds are sold to individuals separately, they are usually accessed through financial advisers, who often have to explain them to consumers while also having to explain how superannuation itself works.

RETIREMENT INCOME PROVIDERS — 131

Retirement funds are those funds that members join following their retirement. These funds can be associated with the fund they were a member of while working, e.g., they might be a sub-division, or they may be totally separate. The main difference for retirement funds is that they are designed to pay you a regular pension or 'income stream' benefit payment, say each month, rather than help you accumulate new superannuation savings.

A note about investment performance information

Each individual super fund supplied the published performance information. To the extent permitted by law, neither *Money*, SelectingSuper, Rainmaker Information Pty Ltd, nor any of their employees, servants or agents warrant the accuracy of any information contained herein, nor does *Money*, SelectingSuper or Rainmaker Information Pty Ltd accept any liability whatsoever (whether arising from negligence, accident or otherwise) for any error contained in the information.

Money, SelectingSuper and Rainmaker Information Pty Ltd recommend that the employer or investor check details of the information provided before making any decisions or relying on the information. Note that past performance is no guarantee to future performance. Rainmaker Information assumes a $50,000 account balance. Your achieved performance may vary based on personal circumstances and additional costs such as insurance etc. may apply; ask your fund for details.

Past performance is no guarantee of future results.

WORKPLACE SUPER PROVIDERS

Workplace super funds are those that are available to employers, whether they are private company or public sector employers. A major feature of these workplace funds is that because they are able to take advantage of the business volume that comes from combining the superannuation buying power of a large number of employees, they often offer wholesale discount fee rates and so are generally cheaper than personal funds.

Aware Super

aware.com.au

Overview

Aware Super is a multi award-winning, profit-to-member industry fund that's been helping members with their superannuation, insurance, advice and retirement solutions for nearly 30 years. As *Money* magazine's 2021 Best Super Fund, Aware Super is recognised for consistent high performance, competitive fees while managing market fluctuations through our investment options.

As one of Australia's largest industry funds, managing $150 billion^ in savings for more than 1.1 million members, Aware Super's scale and skill enables them to adopt innovative, market leading investment strategies - helping members retire with more.

Aware Super has a strong heritage in providing superannuation for NSW and Victorian education, health, emergency services and public sector workers as well as local government workers in WA. Today, they are open to all Australian's and is a fund for community minded people who see no reason to sacrifice integrity for performance – doing well for themselves while doing good for all.

^as at August 2021

FUND VALUE
$150 billion

AT A GLANCE

SPIN FSS0100AU

Year established 1992

Members 1.1 million

Key features

- Profit to member fund operated solely for the benefit of members.
- Great value, with no entry or ongoing contribution fees, no withdrawal fee and no switching fee.
- A range of 12 investment options (including two socially responsible options) offering competitive returns. The High Growth option (default option for members 55 and under) is ranked in the top 10 for performance by Rainmaker Information for 5 and 10 year periods.
- All options have been divested of companies that manufacture cigarettes and tobacco products. All options will also be excluding direct investments in companies deriving 10% or more of their revenues directly from mining thermal or energy coal and companies deriving revenue from the manufacture and/or production of controversial weapons.*
- Member information is readily available and accessible through a variety of channels, including online via our website or app, over

the phone and face to face via our member service centres.
- Flexible insurance options, with automatic death and TPD cover for eligible members. Members can also apply for additional insurance including income protection.
- Comprehensive financial education program including regular regional and workplace seminars as well as educational guides and calculators online.
- All information is provided in plain English to help members understand their super.
- Transition to retirement and retirement income stream products available.
- Full range of advice services from single issue phone advice at no additional fee, through to fee-based comprehensive advice provided by Aware Financial Services Australia Limited, ABN 86 003 742 756, AFSL 238430. Advice can include investment decisions, transition to retirement, insurance, estate planning and aged care services.

Extra benefits available

- Mobile website or app
- Newsletters for members
- Education seminars
- Online account access
- Investment flexibility
- Multi-manager-investment choice(s)
- Ethical/SRI investment choice(s)
- Online investment switching
- Monthly or quarterly investment reports
- Account flexibility
- Retirement products
- Explorer Tool: See how your super is tracking today and how much the retirement lifestyle you want could cost.
- EFT / BPAY contributions
- Binding death benefit nominations

Employer services

- Dedicated employer relationship staff
- Worksite payroll staff training
- Regular employer newsletters
- Helpdesk
- Gateway and clearing house service
- Employer superannuation reference guide
- Face to face employer training sessions
- Employer information seminars

Financial Planning available

- Limited Advice
- Comprehensive Financial Planning

Insurance available

- Death Only
- Combined Death / TPD
- Income Protection

Fees	
Withdrawal fee	$0
Management Cost: member fee ($ per week/annum)	$52 per year plus 0.15% p.a. of account balance, capped at $750 pa.
Management Cost: investment fee (% pa)	0.03% - 1.09%
Switching fee	$0
Other	$0

Investment Performance	Growth Asset Weighting	1yr	3yrs (pa)	5yrs (pa)	10yrs (pa)
Balanced Growth	49.20%	11.32%	6.27%	7.21%	7.08%
Conservative Growth	19.30%	3.96%	3.46%	4.13%	4.73%
Diversified Socially Responsible	65.40%	15.00%	7.78%	7.97%	7.87%
Growth	67.80%	17.77%	8.56%	9.55%	8.72%
High Growth	84.10%	22.87%	10.29%	11.49%	10.36%

Performance to 30 June 2021. Please note that all figures reflect net investment performance, i.e. net of investment tax, investment management fees and the maximum applicable ongoing management and membership fees.

* From 1 October 2020 all options will also be excluding direct investments in companies deriving 10% or more of their revenues directly from mining thermal or energy coal and companies deriving revenue from the manufacture and/or production of controversial weapons including chemical weapons, cluster munitions, land mines and depleted uranium. Due to liquidity constraints, it may take time to divest unlisted thermal coal mining assets and there may be a small residual exposure. Such assets will be sold at fair value as soon as reasonably practicable, but no later than 30 June 2023.

CONTACT

Phone
1300 650 873

Email
enquiries@aware.com.au

SERVICE PROVIDERS

Administrator
Mercer Administration Services (Australia)

Asset consultant
Willis Towers Watson

Auditors
Deloitte

Custodian
State Street Australia Limited

Insurer
TAL Life Limited

BT Super

bt.com.au

FUND VALUE
$18.4 billion*

AT A GLANCE

SPIN BTA0287AU
Year established 2018
Members 292,515*

Overview

From early beginnings, BT has continued to define itself by adapting and responding to customer needs. We have a strong financial services heritage in Australia, giving you the assurance that you are dealing with experienced and knowledgeable experts. We are focused on helping Australians achieve their best financial future forever, by providing customers with a range of wealth services.

These include:

- Investment
- Superannuation
- Insurance solutions

Key features

- Making super simple to manage - anytime, anywhere via the BT member portal and mobile app.
- Side-by-side online access to Westpac customers super accounts via everyday banking to drive stronger member engagement.
- Over 38 investment options from leading global fund managers.
- BT MySuper 'Lifestage' investment option which automatically adjusts the asset mix as members get older.
- MyWellbeing - member access to features: personalised health assessment, recipes, challenges and quizzes to help improve members well-being.

- Access to the 'Benefits Now' program of discounts and offers to help members save money on everyday things.
- Member statements that are clear and highlight important key features such as insurance cover.
- Providing members with a suite of online tools and calculators to make informed decisions about their future.
- SuperCheck enabling members to find their super instantly online.
- Changing jobs functionality – enabling members to trigger a notification to their employer pre-populated with their BT details.

Extra benefits available

Member services:

- Website
- Mobile website or app
- Newsletters for members
- Education seminars

Investment flexibility:

- Investment choice
- Age-based investment choice
- Choice of fund managers

- Ethical/SRI investment choice(s)

Account flexibility:

- Retirement products
- EFT/BPAY contributions
- Contribution splitting
- Binding death benefit nominations
- Non-lapsing binding death benefit nomination

*as at 31 August 2021

Employer services

- Policy Committee report tailored to our employer's needs. Reporting includes market and fund performance, membership and legislative updates.
- Dedicated RG146 complaint Relationship Managers supporting our employers with member education, key account planning and servicing.

- Tailored reporting
- Quicksuper allows our employers to submit obtain payments that are automatically reconcile and processed to members within 1 business day.
- Monthly employer newsletters - legislative and regulatory updates.

Insurance available

- Death Only
- Combined Death / TPD

- Income Protection

Fees	
Entry / joining fee	N/A
Contribution fee	N/A
Exit fee	N/A
Administration fee	$9 per month plus 0.28% of members assets.
Buy-sell spread	This will depend on the investment option chosen.
Switching fee	N/A
Advice fee	N/A
Other	Please refer to the respective fund disclosure material for further details.
Fee Discounts	Some fees outlined above are an estimate only and depend on arrangements with employers.

Investment Performance	Growth Asset Weighting	1yr	3yrs (pa)	5yrs (pa)	10yrs (pa)
BT MySuper - 1940s Lifestage Fund[1]	38	8.36	4.43	3.98	4.22
BT MySuper - 1950s Lifestage Fund[1]	44	10.29	5.05	4.74	5.28
BT MySuper - 1960s Lifestage Fund[1]	59	16.94	6.87	7.06	6.93
BT MySuper - 1970s Lifestage Fund[1]	87	25.52	9.16	9.65	8.58
BT MySuper - 1980s Lifestage Fund[1]	87	25.63	9.23	9.73	8.74
BT MySuper - 1990s Lifestage Fund[1]	87	25.56	9.30	9.86	8.83
BT MySuper - 2000s Lifestage Fund[1]	87	25.10	9.28	9.95	n/a
BT Super - Active Defensive[2]	32	8.42	n/a	n/a	n/a
BT Super - Active Balanced[2]	73	19.38	n/a	n/a	n/a
BT Super - Active Growth[2]	88	23.77	n/a	n/a	n/a

Performance to 30 June 2021.

[1] Performance figures are calculated in accordance with the APRA reporting standards. Total returns are calculated using withdrawal prices appropriate for the month end and take into account management costs and monthly administration fee ($9 per month effective 1 October 2020 and $6.50 per month prior to October 2020) and take into account earnings tax up to a maximum of 15%.

[2] Performance figures are calculated in accordance with the Financial Services Council (FSC) standards. Total returns are calculated using withdrawal prices appropriate for the month end and take into account management costs (other than the monthly administration fee, $9 per month effective 1 October 2020 and $6.50 per month prior to October 2020) and, in the case of Savings investment options only, take into account earnings tax up to a maximum of 15%. In the case of Retirement investment options, no allowance is made for tax you may pay as an investor other than withholding tax on foreign income (if any).

CONTACT

Phone
1300 365 668

Email
customer.relations@
btfinancialgroup.com

SERVICE PROVIDERS

Administrator
In-house administration

Asset consultant
Advance Asset Management Limited

Auditors
PwC

Custodian
HSBC

Insurer
AIA

Lawyer
Allens Linklaters

CareSuper

caresuper.com.au

FUND VALUE
$19 billion

AT A GLANCE

SPIN CAR0100AU
Year established 1986
Members 220,000

Overview

CareSuper is a multi award-winning Industry SuperFund that's been helping members and employers with their super for 35 years. Today, they're one of the largest industry super funds for professionals working across a range of industries. CareSuper's focus is on maximising investment returns for members and delivering superior service so that each of their 220,000 members can achieve their best possible post-work lifestyle.

Working with over 56,000 employers, CareSuper helps businesses stay on top of their super. How? With a streamlined payment system, educational program, seminars and webinars (onsite and virtual) and access to a team of relationship managers who provide personalised support.

For those looking to wind-down or stop work permanently, CareSuper makes it easy to receive a regular income with flexible accounts, including the CareSuper Pension, transition to retirement (TTR) strategy and a Guaranteed Income annuity-type product.

Key features

- As an Industry SuperFund CareSuper is run only to benefit members.
- Active management investment approach has delivered consistently strong performance for members over the long term.*
- Choose from 12 managed investment options, plus a Direct Investment option which offers access to S&P/ ASX 300 Index shares, LICs, ETFs and term deposits (if eligible).
- A dedicated portal for employers to make super payments for all their employees in the one place.
- CareSuper's relationship managers provide dedicated support to employers and staff on all aspects relating to super.
- Financial planning services
- Accumulation, TTR and pension products.

Extra benefits available

- Multi-manager-investment choice(s)
- Ethical / SRI investment choices(s)
- Term deposit investment choice
- Direct shares investment facility
- Online investment switching
- Quarterly and annual investment reports
- Can join without an employer
- Spouse accounts and contribution splitting
- Health, home and travel insurance, and low-cost banking products
- Binding death benefit nominations

Member communications

- Call centre
- Website
- Mobile website or app
- Social media
- Newsletters for members
- Education seminars and webinars
- Online account access
- Online membership application

Employer services

- A clearing house solution allows you to make all employee super contributions in the one place, no matter which fund they're with.
- Quarterly newsletter for employers
- Relationship managers are available to assist employers and employees.
- Workplace seminars and webinars

Insurance available

- Death cover
- Income protection cover
- Total and permanent disablement cover

Fees	
Entry / joining fee	$0
Contribution fee	$0
Administration fee	$78 per year, plus 0.19% of your account balance per year (capped at $750 per annum for super and pension members).
Buy-sell spread	Applies when a member contributes to, or withdraws from all CareSuper's investment options with exception of the Direct Investment option. These fees are reflected in the daily unit prices.
Switching fee	$0, however a buy-sell spread may apply.
Advice fee	$0 for general advice. Fees apply for comprehensive or complex advice.
Other	A monthly admin fee of $10 is payable by members who select the Direct Investment option. Other fees and costs, such as activity fees, advice fees for personal advice or insurance fees, may apply.
Fee Discounts	Nil

Investment Performance	Growth Asset Weighting	1yr	3yrs (pa)	5yrs (pa)	10yrs (pa)
Alternative Growth	68%	15.47%	7.05%	8.44%	8.81%
Australian Shares	100%	27.82%	8.79%	11.36%	9.53%
Balanced	69%	17.49%	7.96%	9.13%	9.13%
Capital Stable	35%	8.22%	4.52%	5.22%	5.98%
Conservative Balanced	50%	11.40%	5.59%	6.56%	7.06%
Direct Property	30%	7.50%	5.81%	8.57%	8.75%
Fixed Interest	Zero	1.15%	3.02%	2.59%	4.39%
Growth	83%	21.32%	8.97%	10.41%	10.08%
Overseas Shares	100%	29.47%	12.85%	13.81%	13.22%
Sustainable Balanced	69%	16.76%	9.23%	9.12%	8.98%

Performance to 30 June 2021. Past performance is not an indication of future performance. Please note that all figures reflect net investment performance, i.e. net of investment fees, indirect costs and tax. There are other investment options available. To view all options, visit caresuper.com.au/investmentoptions. CARE Super Pty Ltd (Trustee) ABN 91 006 670 060 AFSL 235226 CARE Super (Fund) ABN 98 172 275 725.

*Past performance is not a reliable indicator of future performance and should never be the sole factor considered when selecting a fund.

The information provided in this document is general advice only and has been prepared without taking into account your particular financial needs, circumstances or objectives. You should consider your own investment objectives, financial situation and needs and read the appropriate product disclosure statement before making an investment decision. You may also wish to consult a licensed financial adviser.

CONTACT

Phone
1300 360 149

Email
caresuper.com.au/getintouch

SERVICE PROVIDERS

Administrator
Mercer Outsourcing (Australia) Pty Ltd

Asset Consultant
JANA Investment Advisers Pty Ltd

Auditor
PricewaterhouseCoopers (External), KPMG (Internal)

Custodian
JPMorgan Chase Bank, N.A., Sydney Branch, National Australia Bank Asset Servicing, Citigroup Pty Ltd, Sargon CT Pty Ltd

Insurer
MetLife

Lawyer
Greenfields Financial Services Lawyers, Hall & Wilcox Lawyers, Holding Redlich

FUND VALUE
$6.3 billion

AT A GLANCE

SPIN USI EIS0001AU

Year established 1997

Members 20,000

EISS Super

eisuper.com.au

Overview

At EISS Super our members come first. We deliver on our commitment to members - value for money, outstanding service, a focus on long-term investment returns and community involvement. We provide members and employers with quality superannuation, retirement, insurance and financial advice services and are proud to be one of the lowest cost super funds in the market.[1]

Established in 1997, with origins dating back to 1919, we work hard so our members can enjoy the retirement lifestyle they deserve. Historically, EISS Super was exclusively available to the energy industry in NSW. Then in 2013, we opened our fund to everyone so they could join a multi-award winning industry super fund.

Super is a long-term investment and you need a partner that will be there for your employees through every stage of life. Whether they're starting their first job, establishing their career or ready to retire, we're here to help them make the most of their super.

Key features

- Industry super fund, run only to benefit members.
- Open to the public and MySuper[2] authorised so employers can choose us as their default super fund.
- Quality superannuation, retirement, insurance and financial planning services.
- Value for money and one of the lowest cost super funds in the market.[1]
- A focus on long-term investment performance delivered through professionally managed investment options.
- Multi-award winning super fund including a Rainmaker AAA Quality Rating for EISS Super and Pension[3] and Best Value MySuper[2] Product runner up in *Money* Magazine's Best of the Best Awards 2021.
- Online portal or member mobile app account access available 24/7.
- Educational seminars, webinars, calculators and newsletters to help members achieve their retirement goals.
- In-house financial advice team with the knowledge and expertise to help members maximise their super.
- Access to our exclusive member Loyalty Rewards program.

Extra benefits available

- Newsletters for members
- Newsletters for employers
- Education sessions and worksite visits
- Online account access
- Investment choice
- Online and member mobile app investment switching
- Monthly or quarterly investment reports
- Members can join without an employer
- Retirement products
- EFT/BPAY contributions
- Binding death benefit nominations

1 Rainmaker Benchmarking Report, March 2020.

2 Note that our MySuper product did not meet the annual performance assessment for the 7 year period ending 30 June 2021. Visit eisuper.com.au/blog/annual-performance-assessment-result for more information.

3 Rainmaker AAA Quality Rating for EISS Super and EISS Pension 2021.

Employer services

Supporting EISS Super employers is vital to the growth of our fund. We work hard on delivering efficient solutions to enable employers to meet their super obligations with ease such as:

- Super payments made easy with our clearing house solution.
- SuperStream compliant.
- Authorised MySuper[1] fund.

- Support and assistance via our Customer Relationship Managers including workplace sessions designed to help your employees make the most of their super.

Financial advice

- Limited advice
- Full Financial Planning

Insurance available

- Death Only Cover
- Combined Death/TPD Cover
- TPD Only Cover
- Salary Continuance Insurance

Fees	
Entry/joining fee	$0
Contribution fee	$0
Administration fee[2]	Range from 0.21 - 0.39% p.a. depending on the member's investment option.
Investment fee[2]	Range from 0.04 - 0.28% p.a. depending on the member's investment option.
Buy-sell spread	$0
Switching fee	$0
Advice fee	$0
Other[2]	Indirect Cost Ratio (ICR) range from 0.00 - 0.29% p.a. depending on the member's investment option.
Fee Discounts	Nil

Investment Performance	Growth Asset Weighting	1yr	3yrs (pa)	5yrs (pa)	10yrs (pa)
Balanced (MySuper)[1]	71.9%	17.70%	7.06%	7.41%	7.41%
Cash	0.00%	0.30%	0.96%	1.24%	1.82%
Conservative	38.7%	8.35%	4.07%	4.23%	5.03%
High Growth	93.7%	25.84%	9.61%	9.75%	9.01%
Conservative Balanced	55.2%	12.97%	5.31%	5.76%	6.27%

Performance to 30 June 2021. Please note that all figures reflect net investment performance, i.e. net of investment tax, investment management fees and the maximum applicable ongoing management and membership fees. Where past performance information is provided this should not be considered an indication of future performance.

1 Note that our MySuper product did not meet the annual performance assessment for the 7 year period ending 30 June 2021. Visit eisuper.com.au/blog/annual-performance-assessment-result for more information.

2 Fees and costs are deducted from the assets of the investment option and reflected in the daily unit price. The fees and costs are for the financial year ended 30 June 2021 (unless specified otherwise). For further important information about 'Fees and Costs', please refer to the relevant Product Disclosure Statement.

CONTACT

Phone
1300 369 901

Email
contact@eisuper.com.au

SERVICE PROVIDERS

Administrator
Mercer (Australia) Pty Ltd

Asset consultant
JANA Investment Advisers Pty Ltd

Auditor
The Audit Office of New South Wales

Custodian
The Northern Trust Company

Insurer
TAL Life Limited

HESTA

hesta.com.au

FUND VALUE
$64 billion

AT A GLANCE

SPIN HST0100AU
Year established 1987
Members 900,000

Overview

At HESTA, everything we do is to benefit our members.

With more than 900,000 members and $64 billion in funds under management, we've learned a thing or two about looking after super. We're the specialist industry super fund that invests in and for people who make our world better. We're committed to creating better futures for the retirement of our members, women and in fact, all Australians.

We keep member fees down, and our costs low, keeping more of our members' money for their future. We help them take control of their future through education and advice using online tools, nation-wide information sessions or personalised consultations.

Over 30 years of experience in super, combined with our focus on our members' needs and strong long-term performance, has earned us the highest rating from agencies including Rainmaker Information's AAA Quality Rating.

Key features

- Our default option, Balanced Growth, has returned, on average 8.8% p.a.* since inception in 1987.
- We keep our fees down.
- Our Online Portal offers members an easy way to manage their super from their mobile or desktop at their own convenience.
- Eligible members have access to 24/7 protection through default Income Protection Cover and Death Cover.
- We also offer access to lump-sum Total and Permanent Disablement Cover.
- Personalised professional super advice is available to members.

- We provide a range of Ready-Made Investment Options. These include our Sustainable Growth option delivering on average 7.27% p.a. since inception in February 2000 and Indexed balance growth returning 17.13% for the 9 months since inception in October 2021.*
- We also offer a range of Your Choice Asset Classes.
- We are one of the largest investors in renewable energy and climate solutions.
- We are a fund for life – offering both Transition to Retirement and Income Stream options.

Extra benefits available

- Call Centre
- Education seminars
- Online account access
- Online membership application
- Investment Choice
- Ethical / SRI investment choices

- Online education webinars
- Online investment switching
- Can join without an employer
- Retirement products
- Transition to retirement facility
- Binding death benefit nomination

*Past performance is not a reliable indicator of future performance.

Employer services

- QuickSuper – clearing house
- Business Relationship Managers for every state/territory
- Monthly contribution advices
- Quarterly member updates
- Regular employer updates

Insurance available

- Death
- TPD
- Income protection

Fees	
Contribution fee	$0
Administration fee	$1.25 per week, plus 0.08% p.a. – Balanced Growth, or 0.10% p.a – all other options (subject to a fee cap)**
Investment fee	0.67% p.a. — Balanced Growth; 0.02% - 1.16% for other investment options Deducted from investments before earnings are applied
Buy-sell spread	$0
Switching fee	$0
Advice fee	Nil
Other	See Fees and costs at **hesta.com.au/pds** for more information.
Indirect cost ratio	0.14% p.a. — Balanced Growth 0% — 0.27% for other investment options, deducted from investments before earnings are applied.
Fee discounts	Nil

Investment Performance	Growth Asset Weighting		1yr	3yrs (pa)^	5yrs (pa)^
Conservative	Defensive 61%	Growth 39%	8.72%	5.75%	6.18%
Balanced Growth	Defensive 25%	Growth 75%	19.03%	8.48%	9.39%
High Growth	Defensive 10%	Growth 90%	24.92%	10.54%	11.41%
Sustainable Growth	Defensive 25%	Growth 75%	23.03%	11.93%	11.78%
Your Choice	Visit hesta.com.au for details including up-to-date performance.				

**The percentage-based Administration fee is not charged on the amount of the account balance in excess of $350,000.

^Average annual return for the periods

Investment Objective, Performance and Strategic Asset Allocation as at 30 June 2021. The returns shown are net of investment fees, indirect costs and taxes as at 30 June 2021

Product by issued by H.E.S.T. Australia Ltd ABN 66 006 818 695 AFSL 235249, the Trustee of Health Employees Superannuation Trust Australia (HESTA) ABN 64 971 749 321.

This information is of a general nature. It does not take into account your objectives, financial situation or specific needs so you should look at your own financial position and requirements before making a decision. You may wish to consult an adviser when doing this. The target market determination for HESTA products can be found at hesta.com.au/tmd Before making a decision about HESTA products you should read the relevant Product Disclosure Statement (call 1800 813 327 or visit hesta.com.au for a copy), and consider any relevant risk (visit the HESTA website for more information).

CONTACT

Phone
1800 813 327

Email
hesta@hesta.com.au

SERVICE PROVIDERS

Administrator
Australian Administration Services Pty Ltd (Part of Link Group)

Asset consultant
Frontier Advisors Pty Ltd

Auditor
PwC, KPMG

Custodian
JPMorgan Chase Bank

Insurer
AIA Australia

Lawyers
Allens Linklaters, HWL Ebsworth

Technology Providers
Tecala Group Pty Ltd

Hostplus Industry

hostplus.com.au

FUND VALUE
$66 billion

AT A GLANCE

SPIN HOS0100AU

Year established 1988

Members 1.3 million

Overview

Hostplus is the national superannuation fund for the hospitality, tourism, recreation and sport industries. We have over 1.3 million members, 236,000 employers and over $66 billion in funds under management. Hostplus is run to benefit members, so there are no commissions paid to financial advisers and no dividends are paid to shareholders.

Key features

- **Consistent long-term investment performance** – We aim to achieve competitive, long-term investment performance for members.
- **Choose your investment strategy** – Hostplus offers a wide range of investment options to suit your needs.
- **Choiceplus investment option** – Invest in Term Deposits, ETFs, LICs and Australian Shares (S&P/ASX 300 Index).
- **Socially Responsible investment option** – meets standards in environmental performance, social impact, ethics, labour standards and corporate governance.
- **Online access** – With Member Online you can update your details, investment choice and apply to change your insurance.

- **Hostplus Pension** – Continue to enjoy all the benefits of being a Hostplus member in retirement.
- **Insurance for peace of mind** – Death and Total & Permanent Disability, Death only and Salary Continuance Cover.
- **Run to benefit members** – We don't pay dividends to shareholders like retail funds.
- **Low administration fees** – Members pay a low administration fee of $1.50 per week, unchanged since 2004.
- **Hostplus digital member card** – Your super fund details in one convenient member card on your phone.

Extra benefits available

- Call Centre
- Website
- Online account access and App
- Online membership application
- Investment Choice
- Age-based investment choice

- Ethical/SRI investment choice(s)
- Online investment switching
- Retirement products
- Transition to retirement facility
- EFT/BPAY contributions
- Binding death benefit nominations

Employer services

No fees. Easy payments. On-call assistance. We'll keep you up to date on the issues that matter, including your employer obligations and any changes to super rules. Visit hostplus.com.au to join us.

Financial advice

- Full Financial Advice available on fee basis

Insurance available

- Death Only
- Death/TPD
- Income Protection

Fees	
Entry/ joining fee	Nil
Contribution fee	Nil
Administration fee	$1.50 per week.
Buy-sell spread	Nil
Switching fee	Nil
Advice fee	Nil
Other	Other fees and costs may apply, such as activity fees, advice fees for personal advice, insurance fees and Choiceplus investment option fees.
Investment fee	Investment fees and costs which vary according to your chosen investment option.

Investment Performance	Growth Asset Weighting	1yr	3yrs (pa)	5yrs (pa)	10yrs (pa)
Australian Shares	100%	28.74%	9.11%	11.45%	10.11%
Balanced	76%	21.32%	8.33%	10.12%	9.67%
Capital Stable	35%	8.61%	3.51%	5.05%	5.74%
Cash	0%	0.07%	0.95%	1.14%	1.85%
Conservative Balanced	55%	14.19%	6.19%	7.70%	7.61%
Diversified Fixed Interest	0%	-0.40%	2.82%	3.33%	5.42%
Indexed Balanced	75%	18.88%	8.92%	9.33%	9.20%
Infrastructure	60%	8.49%	N/A	N/A	N/A
International Shares	100%	30.15%	13.71%	15.48%	12.22%
International Shares - Indexed	100%	24.57%	13.07%	N/A	N/A
International Shares (Hedged) - Indexed	100%	30.28%	12.46%	N/A	N/A
Property	30%	7.78%	5.23%	7.22%	7.55%
Shares Plus	89%	26.00%	10.52%	12.28%	10.64%
Socially Responsible Investment (SRI) – Balanced	74%	21.82%	8.85%	N/A	N/A

The Growth Asset Weightings (GAW) above reflect Rainmaker's classifications that are assigned to each asset class. GAWs reflected may differ from what is disclosed directly by the product provider.

Performance to 30 June 2021. Please note that all performance figures reflect net investment performance (i.e. net of investment tax, investment management fees and costs).

CONTACT

Phone
1300 467 875

Email
info@hostplus.com.au

SERVICE PROVIDERS

Administrator
AAS

Asset consultant
JANA Investment Advisers

Custodians
Citigroup Pty Limited, Pacific Custodians Pty Limited

Insurer
MetLife

Lawyers
Mills Oakley Lawyers, Holding Redlich

FUND VALUE
$26 billion

AT A GLANCE

SPIN MTA0100AU
Year established 1989
Members 321,000

Spirit Super

spiritsuper.com.au

Overview

Spirit Super is a multi-industry super fund with $26 billion funds under management and over 321,000 members across Australia. We're here to help everyday Australians get the most out of their super through competitive investment returns and low fees. We take great pride in offering excellent service no matter your life stage or retirement goals. It all starts with spirit.

Key features

- An industry super fund with a strong member focus. With offices across the country, Spirit Super prides itself on excellent service, personalised advice[1] and support you can count on.
- Committed to a low-cost fee structure. All profits are returned to members.
- Flexible insurance options, offering protection for you and your loved ones.
- A range of pre-mixed and asset class investment options to choose from.
- The ability to provide you with general and intra-fund advice (at no extra cost), and set fees to provide you with comprehensive advice.
- Product offers taking you from accumulation to retirement, and access to member-only benefits.

Extra benefits available

Member services:
- Call centre
- Newsletters for members
- Education seminars
- Mobile website or app

Investment flexibility:
- Investment choice
- Online investment switching

- Monthly or quarterly investment reports
- Ethical/SRI investment choice

Account flexibility:
- Retirement products
- Transition to retirement facility
- BPAY contributions
- Contribution splitting
- Binding death benefit nominations

Financial planning available[1]

- Limited Advice
- Full Financial Planning

Employer services

Free clearing house facilities, employer and employee workshops and webinars, experienced staff to support employers, regular updates.

Insurance available

- Death cover (including terminal illness)
- Income protection cover
- Total and permanent disablement (TPD) cover
- Default and voluntary cover options

Fees[2]	
Entry/joining fee	$0
Contribution fee	$0
Administration fee	$67.60 plus 0.15% of your account balance each year (the percentage fee is capped at $450 each year).
Investment fee	Conservative – 0.51% Cash – 0.05% Moderate – 0.59% Diversified fixed interest – 0.30% Balanced (MySuper) – 0.74% Australian shares – 0.84% Sustainable – 0.91% International shares – 0.78% Growth – 0.81%
Buy-sell spread	$0
Switching fee	$0
Advice fee	$0 Fees for general and intra-fund advice are included as part of the administration fee
Other	Other fees and costs, such as activity fees, advice fees for personal advice and insurance fees, may be charged, but these will depend on the nature of the activity, advice or insurance you choose. For more information, refer to Additional explanation of fees and costs section in Fees and costs available at spiritsuper.com.au/pds.

Investment Performance[3]	Growth Asset Weighting	1yr	3yrs (pa)	5yrs (pa)	10yrs (pa)
Conservative		6.49%	4.20%	4.72%	4.04%
Moderate*		10.04%	6.34%	6.36%	NA
Balanced (MySuper)		17.43%	7.79%	8.74%	8.19%
Sustainable*		15.03%	7.99%	8.51%	NA
Growth		21.97%	9.34%	10.61%	9.04%
Australian shares		24.82%	8.72%	11.01%	9.34%
International shares		30.25%	11.13%	12.29%	10.94%
Diversified fixed interest		0.61%	2.74%	2.37%	3.69%
Cash		0.22%	0.99%	1.27%	1.94%

[2] Fees and returns are for Spirit Super accumulation accounts.

If your Spirit Super account balance is less than $6,000 at 30 June each year or when you close your account, the total combined amount of administration fees, investment fees and indirect costs charged to you is capped at 3% of your account balance. Any amount charged in excess of that cap must be refunded. If you hold more than one account with us, we'll assess each account separately.

Investment fees are estimates of what the likely ongoing investment fees will be based on information available to us when preparing this table. For further information, see our Fees and costs information sheet at spiritsuper.com.au/pds. The actual investment fees for the current financial year may vary due to changes to the underlying investments.

[3] Performance as at 30 June 2021.

The figures shown are net investment returns, that is, after fees, costs and taxes have been paid.

Past performance isn't necessarily an indication of future returns.

Crediting rates with MTAA Super prior to 2017 have been converted to unit prices. Before 22 April 2017, MTAA Super used crediting rates to apply the returns for investment options to members.

*Investment performance shown up to 31 March 2021 is for Tasplan investment options.

CONTACT

Phone
1800 005 166

Email
info@spiritsuper.com.au

SERVICE PROVIDERS

Administrator
In-house

Asset consultant
Whitehelm Capital Pty Ltd

External auditor
PricewaterhouseCoopers

Internal auditor
Deloitte

Custodians
NAB Asset Servicing
(a division of the National Australia Bank)

Insurer
MetLife Insurance Limited

FirstChoice Employer Super

www.cfs.com.au/employer

FUND VALUE
Nearly $15 billion

CONTACT

Phone
1300 654 666

Email
employer@cfs.com.au

AT A GLANCE

SPIN USI FSF0361AU

Year established 2002

Members Over 210,000

SERVICE PROVIDERS

Administrator
Colonial First State Investments
Limited (CFSIL)

Asset consultant Mercer

Auditor
PriceWaterhouseCoopers

Custodians
Citi, Bank of New York, Northern
Trust

Insurer
AIA Australia Limited

Overview

FirstChoice Employer Super is a highly rated[1] fund that gives members access to a wide range of investments, with tailored insurance options and negotiated administration fees. It is a fund designed and delivered by experts in super and retirement planning with nearly $15 billion invested on behalf of over 210,000[1] Australians.

Key features

- **Award winning** – Our experienced national teams is dedicated to providing the very best employer and member education and investment support.
- **The MySuper Lifestage default investment** – an investment option designed to automatically adjust how it invests throughout a member's working life to suit their changing needs.
- **Negotiated administration fees** – available to some employers to benefit your members.
- **Flexible insurance options** – Members can take advantage of Death, Total and Permanent Disablement cover (TPD) and Salary Continuance Insurance (SCI)*.
  *There are rules around when automatic insurance can be provided to members. Generally, members are eligible when they reach age 25 and their super account balance reaches $6000.

Investment Performance	1yr	3yrs	5yrs	Since inception[2]
FirstChoice Lifestage (1950-1954)	9.21%	4.37%	4.69%	5.13%
FirstChoice Lifestage (1955-1959)	9.40%	4.40%	4.85%	5.60%
FirstChoice Lifestage (1960-1964)	13.44%	5.27%	6.55%	7.07%
FirstChoice Lifestage (1965-1969)	21.14%	6.94%	8.51%	8.39%
FirstChoice Lifestage (1970-1974)	24.54%	7.81%	9.09%	8.73%
FirstChoice Lifestage (1975-1979)	25.59%	7.98%	9.20%	8.73%
FirstChoice Lifestage (1980-1984)	25.83%	8.03%	9.23%	8.76%
FirstChoice Lifestage (1985-1989)	25.83%	8.05%	9.24%	8.78%
FirstChoice Lifestage (1990-1994)	25.64%	8.00%	9.21%	8.76%
FirstChoice Lifestage (1995-1999)	25.44%	8.06%	9.26%	8.82%
FirstChoice Lifestage (2000-2004)	25.36%	7.98%	9.15%	9.51%

[1] FirstChoice Employer Super has been awarded AAA Quality Rating from Rainmaker Information, from 2008-2021.

[2] As at June 2021

Performance shown is for periods to 30 June 2021 after percentage based fees and taxes. Past performance is not an indicator of future performance. For more information, visit www.colonialfirststate.com.au/employerperformance.

Maritime Super

maritimesuper.com.au

Overview

Maritime Super is the largest industry fund for the maritime industry. We're one of Australia's longest running super funds. We've delivered innovative super and retirement benefits to generations of members for over 50 years. With a national presence, we offer personalised service through member engagement programs that include welcome calls and worksite visits across the country.

Maritime Super offers a range of diversified and sector investment options invested in the Hostplus Pooled Superannuation Trust, part of a larger asset pool of over $70 billion. Our goal is to help members make the right decisions now to secure financial freedom in the future.

Key features

- Profit-for-members philosophy – as an industry fund, we are run only for the benefit of members.
- Investment performance – our investment strategy is focused on delivering long-term investment growth.
- Range of investment options – we offer a range of diversified and sector investment options to members.
- Member services – exceptional support, we don't time calls, we spend as long as it takes to help.
- Quality member education – we help you make informed decisions about super through a range of member communications.
- Insurance protection – access to comprehensive insurance cover, tailored to maritime occupations and risks.
- Access to financial advice - national network of financial planners operate on a fee-for-service basis with no commissions.
- Pension options - we offer a range of pension products, including allocated pension and transition to retirement pension.

FUND VALUE
$6 billion

CONTACT

Phone
1800 757 607

Email
info@
maritimesuper.com.au

AT A GLANCE

SPIN MSL0001AU

Year established 1967

Members 25,000

SERVICE PROVIDERS

Administrator
Maritime Financial Services
Pty Limited

Asset consultant
Frontier Advisers

Auditor
Ernst & Young

Custodian
Citigroup Pty Limited

Insurer
MLC Limited

Lawyer
Allens

Active Super

activesuper.com.au

FUND VALUE
$7.2 billion

CONTACT

Phone
1300 467 875

Email
hello@activesuper.com.au

Overview

Active Super, formerly known as Local Government Super, manages more than $14 billion in superannuation assets for over 80,000 members, including current and former NSW local government employees. We hold investments across Australian and international shares, property, infrastructure, private equity, fixed interest and absolute return asset classes.

We were named a Leader in Responsible Investment by the Responsible Investment Association Australasia in its 2021 Benchmark Report. Plus, we've won the SuperRatings Infinity Award for leading the industry in responsible investment for a record seven times.

At a glance

SPIN LGS0101AU
Year established 1997
Members 80,000

Key features

- A members-first industry fund, with profits returned to members.
- A range of investment choices with sustainable long-term performance.
- Flexible insurance, including death, TPD and salary continuance.
- Convenient account access via Member Online or mobile app.
- Workplace seminars, education and financial planning services.
- Discounted health insurance offers through HCF.

LUCRF Super

lucrf.com.au

FUND VALUE
$7.4 billion

CONTACT

Phone
1300 130 780

Email
mypartner@lucrf.com.au

Overview

LUCRF Super is an industry super fund that works hard for your future. We work to support our members, for change in the community, and for a better financial future for all. We offer a range of high quality, award-winning superannuation, pension and insurance products to our members, and strive to deliver consistently competitive returns and friendly service at minimal cost. We also provide members with access to financial advice and retirement seminars and webinars.

At a glance

SPIN LUC0001AU
Year established 1978
Members 125,700+

Key features

- Solid long-term investment returns.
- Competitive fees.
- Wide range of investment options.
- Personalised financial advice and educational seminars and webinars.
- In-house contact centre.
- Flexible insurance.

Workplace Super Providers

Includes (a selection of corporate funds, Industry funds, Government funds and Corporate master trusts)

Active Super Defined Benefit Scheme	1300 547 873	activesuper.com.au
Acumen	1300 305 779	rest.com.au/member/products/REST-Acumen
Alcoa of Australia Retirement Plan - Accumulation	1800 355 028	alcoasuper.com.au
Alcoa of Australia Retirement Plan - Defined Benefit	1800 355 028	alcoasuper.com.au
AMG Core Super	1300 264 264	amgsuper.com.au/products
AMG Corporate Super	1300 264 264	amgsuper.com.au/products
AMIST Super Employer Sponsored Division	1800 808 614	amist.com.au
AMP CustomSuper	1300 653 456	amp.com.au
AMP Flexible Super - Employer Plan	131 267	amp.com.au
AMP SignatureSuper	1300 366 019	amp.com.au
AMP SignatureSuper Select	1300 366 019	amp.com.au
AMP SuperLeader	1300 558 557	amp.com.au
ANZ Australian Staff Superannuation Scheme - Employee Section	1800 000 086	anzstaffsuper.com
ANZ Smart Choice Super - Employer	131 287	anz.com.au
ANZ Super Advantage	133 863	anz.com.au
Aon Master Trust - Corporate	1300 880 588	smartmonday.com.au
ARC Master Trust Corporate	1300 209 088	arcmt.com.au
Asgard Corporate Superannuation Service	1800 998 185	asgard.com.au
Asgard Employee Super Account	1800 998 185	asgard.com.au/products-and-services/business-super
AustChoice Super Employer Division	1800 333 900	austchoice.com.au/super/product_information/Super_division
Australia Post Superannuation Scheme - Defined Benefit	1300 360 373	apss.com.au
Australia Post Superannuation Scheme - Member Savings	1300 360 373	apss.com.au
Australian Catholic Superannuation - Employer Sponsored Plan	1300 658 776	catholicsuper.com.au
Australian Defence Force Superannuation Scheme	1300 203 439	adfsuper.gov.au
Australian Ethical Retail Superannuation Fund - Employer	1300 134 337	australianethical.com.au
AustralianSuper	1300 300 273	australiansuper.com
AustralianSuper Corporate Solutions	1300 300 273	australiansuper.com
AvSuper Corporate	1800 805 088	avsuper.com.au
AvSuper Defined Benefit	1800 805 088	avsuper.com.au
Aware Super - Ambulance	1300 650 873	aware.com.au
Aware Super - Police Blue Ribbon Super	1300 650 873	aware.com.au
Bendigo SmartStart Super - Employer	1800 033 426	sandhursttrustees.com.au/smartstart
BOC Gases Superannuation Fund	1300 136 829	bocsuper.com.au
BT Lifetime Super Employer Plan	132 135	bt.com.au
BUSSQ MySuper	1800 657 216	bussq.com.au
Catholic Super	1300 550 273	csf.com.au
Cbus Corporate Super	1300 361 784	cbussuper.com.au
Cbus Industry Super	1300 361 784	cbussuper.com.au

Child Care Super	1800 060 215	childcaresuper.com.au
Christian Super	1300 360 907	christiansuper.com.au
Citibank Australia Staff Superannuation Fund	1800 127 953	super.towerswatson.com/super/citi
Club Plus Industry Division	1800 680 627	clubplussuper.com.au
Colonial Select Corporate Superannuation	1300 550 552	
Colonial SuperChoice Corporate Super	1800 805 898	
Commonwealth Bank Group Super - Accumulate Plus	1800 023 928	oursuperfund.com.au
Commonwealth Bank Group Super - Defined Benefit	1800 023 928	oursuperfund.com.au
Commonwealth Superannuation Scheme	1300 000 277	csc.gov.au
Commonwealth SuperSelect	132 221	commbank.com.au
EISS Defined Benefit Scheme	1300 369 901	eisuper.com.au
Electricity Industry Superannuation Scheme	1300 307 844	electricsuper.com.au
Energy Super	1300 363 240	energysuper.com.au
Energy Super - Defined Benefit	1300 363 240	energysuper.com.au
Enterprise Super - Employer Sponsored	1800 816 575	
Equip Corporate	03 9248 5940	equipsuper.com.au
Equip MyFuture	1800 682 626	equipsuper.com.au
Equipsuper - Defined Benefit	1800 682 626	equipsuper.com.au
Essential Super - Employer	134 074	commbank.com.au/super-retiring/essential-super
ESSS Defined Benefit Fund	1300 650 161	esssuper.com.au
ESSS State Super Defined Benefit Fund	1300 650 161	esssuper.com.au
ESSSuper Beneficiary Account	1300 650 161	esssuper.com.au
Fiducian Corporate Superannuation	1800 653 263	fiducian.com.au/superannuation
Fire and Emergency Services Superannuation Fund	08 9382 8444	fessuper.com.au
First Super - Employer Sponsored	1300 360 988	firstsuper.com.au
GESB Gold State Super	134 372	gesb.com.au
GESB Super	134 372	gesb.com.au
GESB West State Super	134 372	gesb.com.au
GROW Super		onesuper.com/funds/grow
GuildSuper	1300 361 477	guildsuper.com.au
Holden Employees Superannuation Fund	1800 700 995	holdensuper.com.au
Holden Employees Superannuation Fund - Defined Benefit	1800 700 995	holdensuper.com.au
Hostplus Executive	1300 467 875	hostplus.com.au/executive
Integra Super (Corporate Division)	133 665	onepath.com.au/superandinvestment/integra-super
Intrust Super - Core Super	132 467	intrustsuper.com.au
Intrust Super - Executive Super	132 467	intrustsuper.com.au
IOOF Employer Super - Employer	1800 333 500	ioof.com.au
legalsuper	1800 060 312	legalsuper.com.au
LESF and Macmahon Super	1800 359 686	onesuper.com/funds/lesf-macmahon-super
LGIAsuper Accumulation	1800 444 396	lgiasuper.com.au
LifeTrack Corporate Superannuation	1800 653 894	ioof.com.au

LifeTrack Employer Superannuation	1300 653 455	ioof.com.au
Local Government Superannuation Scheme (QLD) - Defined Benefit Account	1800 444 396	lgiasuper.com.au
Local Government Superannuation Scheme (QLD) - Defined Benefit Fund	1800 444 396	lgiasuper.com.au
Lutheran Super	1800 635 796	lutheransuper.com.au
Lutheran Super - Defined Benefit	1800 635 796	lutheransuper.com.au
max Super for Business	1300 629 727	onesuper.com/funds/max-super
Meat Industry Employees' Superannuation Fund	1800 252 099	miesf.com.au
Media Super	1800 640 886	mediasuper.com.au
Medical & Associated Professions Superannuation - Employer Division	1800 333 500	mapsuper.com.au
Mercer Super Trust - Corporate Super Division	1800 682 525	mercerfinancialservices.com
Mercer Super Trust - SmartSuper Plan Individual Section	1800 682 525	mercerfinancialservices.com
Mercy Super	1300 368 891	mercysuper.com.au
Mercy Super - Defined Benefit	1300 368 891	mercysuper.com.au
Military Super	1300 006 727	csc.gov.au
Mine Super	13 64 63	mine.com.au
MLC MasterKey Business Super	132 652	mlc.com.au
MLC Navigator Retirement Plan Series 2 - Superannuation Service	132 652	mlc.com.au
MyLife MySuper Employer Sponsored	1300 695 433	mylifemysuper.com.au
National Australia Bank Group Superannuation Fund "A"	1300 557 586	nabgsf.com.au
Nationwide Super Employer Division	1800 025 241	nationwidesuper.com.au
NESS Super	1800 022 067	nesssuper.com.au
netwealth Super Accelerator Employer Sponsored Super	1800 888 223	netwealth.com.au
NGS Super Accumulation	1300 133 177	ngssuper.com.au
Northern Territory Government and Public Authorities Superannuation Scheme	1800 631 630	nt.gov.au/ntt/super
Northern Territory Supplementary Superannuation Scheme	1800 631 630	nt.gov.au/ntt/super
Plum Superannuation Fund Employer Division	1300 557 586	plum.com.au
PortfolioCare Super Service Employer Account	1800 646 234	amp.com.au
Prime Super (Health Division)	1800 675 839	primesuper.com.au
Prime Super (Prime Division)	1800 675 839	primesuper.com.au
Prime Super Education Division	1800 675 839	primesuper.com.au
Progress Super Fund - Corporate	1300 880 736	
Public Sector Superannuation accumulation plan	1300 725 171	csc.gov.au
Public Sector Superannuation Scheme	1300 000 377	csc.gov.au
Qantas Superannuation Plan	1300 362 967	qantassuper.com.au
Qantas Superannuation Plan - Defined Benefit	1300 362 967	qantassuper.com.au
Qantas Superannuation Plan - Gateway	1300 362 967	qantassuper.com.au
QSuper Accumulation Account	1300 360 750	qsuper.qld.gov.au
QSuper Defined Benefit Account	1300 360 750	qsuper.qld.gov.au
REI Super	1300 134 433	reisuper.com.au
Resource Super Employer Division	1800 555 667	resourcesuper.com.au
Rest Corporate	1300 300 778	rest.com.au/member/products/rest-corporate

Rest Super	1300 300 778	rest.com.au/member/products/rest-super
Russell iQ Super Employer	1800 555 667	russellinvestments.com/au/solutions/iq-super-employer/overview
SA Ambulance Service Superannuation Scheme	1300 364 941	ambsuper.sa.gov.au
SA Governors Pension Scheme	08 8226 9839	supersa.gov.au
SA Judges' Pension Scheme	08 8226 9839	supersa.sa.gov.au
SA Metropolitan Fire Service Superannuation Scheme	08 8204 3826	samfs.superfacts.com
SA Parliamentary Superannuation Scheme	08 8226 9839	supersa.sa.gov.au
SA Parliamentary Superannuation Scheme 3	08 8207 2094	supersa.sa.gov.au
SA Police Superannuation Fund - Old (Pension) Scheme Division	08 8204 2964	policesuper.sa.gov.au
SA Police Superannuation Scheme - Police Employer Account	08 8204 2964	policesuper.sa.gov.au
SA State Lump Sum Scheme	1300 369 315	supersa.sa.gov.au/our_products/lump_sum_scheme
SA State Pension Scheme	1300 369 315	supersa.sa.gov.au/our_products/pension_scheme
smartMonday PRIME	1300 880 588	smartmonday.com.au
smartMonday PRIME TESF	1300 614 644	smartmonday.com.au
Smartsave Employer Super	1300 654 720	onesuper.com/funds/smartsave
Southern State Superannuation Scheme	1300 369 315	supersa.sa.gov.au/our_products/triple_s
State Super (NSW) - Police Superannuation Scheme	1300 130 097	statesuper.nsw.gov.au/pss
State Super (NSW) - State Authorities Non-Contributory Superannuation Scheme	1300 130 096	statesuper.nsw.gov.au
State Super (NSW) - State Authorities Superannuation Scheme	1300 130 095	statesuper.nsw.gov.au/sass
State Super (NSW) - State Superannuation Scheme	1300 130 096	statesuper.nsw.gov.au/sss
StatewideSuper	1300 651 865	statewide.com.au
StatewideSuper Defined Benefit	1300 651 865	statewide.com.au
SUMMIT Master Trust Employer Sponsored Super Plan	1800 667 841	northonline.com.au/summit
Suncorp Brighter Super for Business	13 11 55	suncorp.com.au
Suncorp Everyday Super for business	13 11 55	suncorp.com.au
Sunsuper for Life - Super-Savings Account	131 184	sunsuper.com.au
Sunsuper for Life Business	131 184	sunsuper.com.au
Sunsuper for Life Corporate	131 184	sunsuper.com.au
Super SA Select	1300 137 668	supersa.sa.gov.au
Telstra Super Corporate Plus	1800 033 166	telstrasuper.com.au
Telstra Superannuation Scheme - Defined Benefit	1800 033 166	telstrasuper.com.au
Tidswell Master Super Plan	08 8223 1676	tidswell.com.au
Toyota Super	1800 700 884	toyotasuper.com.au
Toyota Super - Defined Benefit	1800 700 884	toyotasuper.com.au
TWUSUPER	1800 222 071	twusuper.com.au
UniSuper	1800 331 685	unisuper.com.au
UniSuper - Defined Benefit Division	1800 331 685	unisuper.com.au
VicSuper FutureSaver	1300 366 216	vicsuper.com.au
Virgin Money Super Employer Division	1300 652 770	virginmoney.com.au/superannuation
Vision Super - Defined Benefit	1300 300 820	visionsuper.com.au
Vision Super Saver	1300 300 820	visionsuper.com.au
VISSF Accumulation	1300 660 027	vissf.com.au

PERSONAL SUPER PROVIDERS

Personal super funds are those that are available to individual consumers. Because personal super funds are sold to individual consumers rather than to larger scale workplaces, they will usually have to charge fees that are higher than workplace funds. And, because these funds are sold to individuals separately, they are usually accessed through financial advisers, who often have to explain them to consumers while also having to explain how superannuation itself works.

FUND VALUE
$150 billion

AT A GLANCE

SPIN FSS0100AU

Year established 1992

Members 1.1 million

Aware Super

aware.com.au

Overview

Aware Super is a multi award-winning, profit-to-member industry fund that's been helping members with their superannuation, insurance, advice and retirement solutions for nearly 30 years. As *Money* magazine's 2021 Best Super Fund, Aware Super is recognised for consistent high performance, competitive fees while managing market fluctuations through our investment options.

As one of Australia's largest industry funds, managing $150 billion^ in savings for more than 1.1 million members. Aware Super's scale and skill enables them to adopt innovative, market leading investment strategies - helping members retire with more.

Aware Super has a strong heritage in providing superannuation for NSW and Victorian education, health, emergency services and public sector workers as well as local government workers in WA. Today, they are open to all Australian's and is a fund for community minded people who see no reason to sacrifice integrity for performance – doing well for themselves while doing good for all.

^as at August 2021

Key features

- Profit to member fund operated solely for the benefit of members.
- Great value, with no entry or ongoing contribution fees, no withdrawal fee and no switching fee.
- A range of 12 investment options (including two socially responsible options) offering competitive returns. The High Growth option (default option for members 55 and under) is ranked in the top 10 for performance by Rainmaker Information for 5 and 10 year periods.
- All options have been divested of companies that manufacture cigarettes and tobacco products. All options will also be excluding direct investments in companies deriving 10% or more of their revenues directly from mining thermal or energy coal and companies deriving revenue from the manufacture and/or production of controversial weapons.*
- Member information is readily available and accessible through a variety of channels, including online via our website or app, over

the phone and face to face via our member service centres
- Flexible insurance options, with death, TPD and income protection cover available for eligible members.
- Comprehensive financial education program including regular regional and workplace seminars as well as educational guides and calculators online.
- All information is provided in plain English to help members understand their super.
- Transition to retirement and retirement income stream products available.
- Full range of advice services from single issue phone advice at no additional fee, through to fee-based comprehensive advice provided by Aware Financial Services Australia Limited, ABN 86 003 742 756, AFSL 238430. Advice can include investment decisions, transition to retirement, insurance, estate planning and aged care services.

Extra benefits available

- Mobile website or app
- Newsletters for members
- Education seminars
- Investment choice
- Multi-manager investment choice(s)
- Age-based investment choice
- Choice of asset allocation
- Ethical / SRI investment choice(s)
- Online investment switching
- Monthly or quarterly investment reports
- Can join without employer
- Spouse accounts
- Retirement products
- Explorer Tool: See how your super is tracking today and how much the retirement lifestyle you want could cost.
- EFT / BPAY contributions
- Contribution splitting
- Binding death benefit nominations

Financial Planning available

- Limited Advice
- Comprehensive Financial Planning

Insurance available

- Death Only
- Combined Death / TPD
- Income Protection

Fees	
Withdrawal fee	$0
Management Cost: member fee ($ per week/annum)	$52 per year plus 0.15% p.a. of account balance, capped at $750 pa.
Management Cost: investment fee (% pa)	0.03% - 1.09%
Switching fee	$0
Other	$0

Investment Performance	Growth Asset Weighting	1yr	3yrs (pa)	5yrs (pa)	10yrs (pa)
Balanced Growth	49.20%	11.32%	6.27%	7.21%	7.08%
Conservative Growth	19.30%	3.96%	3.46%	4.13%	4.73%
Diversified Socially Responsible	65.40%	15.00%	7.78%	7.97%	7.87%
Growth	67.80%	17.77%	8.56%	9.55%	8.72%
High Growth	84.10%	22.87%	10.29%	11.49%	10.36%

Performance to 30 June 2021. Please note that all figures reflect net investment performance, i.e. net of investment tax, investment management fees and the maximum applicable ongoing management and membership fees.

* From 1 October 2020 all options will also be excluding direct investments in companies deriving 10% or more of their revenues directly from mining thermal or energy coal and companies deriving revenue from the manufacture and/or production of controversial weapons including chemical weapons, cluster munitions, land mines and depleted uranium. Due to liquidity constraints, it may take time to divest unlisted thermal coal mining assets and there may be a small residual exposure. Such assets will be sold at fair value as soon as reasonably practicable, but no later than 30 June 2023.

CONTACT

Phone
1300 650 873

Email
enquiries@aware.com.au

SERVICE PROVIDERS

Administrator
Mercer Administration Services (Australia)

Asset consultant
Willis Towers Watson

Auditors
Deloitte

Custodian
State Street Australia Limited

Insurer
TAL Life Limited

FUND VALUE
$100 billion

AT A GLANCE

SPIN UNI0001AU

Year established 1982

Members More than 450,000

UniSuper Personal Account

unisuper.com.au

Overview

UniSuper is one of Australia's largest super funds and is run in the best interests of its members. Over 450,000 Australian's trust us with their retirement savings, enjoying our record of low fees, strong long-term performance across various investment options* and commitment to sustainable investment. With over $100 billion in funds under management, we're passionate about securing the future of our members, sharing in a wealth of wisdom and collective know-how. We empower members to be confident to make better financial decisions and create a future worth retiring for.

Key features

- Industry super fund open to all Australians.
- More than 70% of funds managed in-house by our investments team.
- A range of investment options, including sustainable and environmental options.
- Run in the best interests of members, we don't pay profits to shareholders or commissions to advisers.
- Administration fees that are among the lowest in the industry.
- An award winning fund as voted by Australia's top ratings and research agencies.

- Affordable and flexible insurance options available through your super.
- Access to free learning resources - online and in person.
- Easy, quick and secure access to an online account.
- Regular member statements that highlight investment options and performance, insurance cover and other important information related to a UniSuper account.
- Easy to use online calculators and tools to help members understand, plan and manage their super.

Employer services

- Committed to delivering exceptional services for our employers to help make super obligations easier.
- Dedicated employer services team to support day-to-day operations, provide information about how super works and process the required super obligations.
- Easy to access forms, guides and frequently asked questions.

- Regular employer newsletter to provide updates and information on how we assist our employers.
- Quick and secure access to Employer Online.
- An easy-to-use system to submit contributions and data online.
- The confidence your employees are in good hands.

Fees	
Entry/joining fee	N/A
Contribution fee	N/A
Administration fee	The lesser of $96 per annum ($8.00 per month, deducted monthly) or 2% of account balance per year
Buy-sell spread	N/A
Switching fee	The first switch each financial year is free, each subsequent switch is $9.85.
Advice fee	Select Advice: Up to $120 per hour (including GST); Comprehensive Advice: $310 per hour (including GST). UniSuper does not pay adviser fees or commissions.

Investment Performance#	1yr	3yrs (pa)	5yrs (pa)	10yrs (pa)
Sustainable High Growth	24.57%	13.94%	13.17%	11.71%
High Growth	27.95%	12.30%	13.48%	11.78%
Growth	23.48%	10.73%	11.47%	10.65%
Sustainable Balanced	17.08%	10.94%	10.23%	9.57%
Balanced	17.60%	9.23%	9.55%	9.55%
Conservative Balanced	7.45%	5.27%	5.30%	7.15%
Conservative	4.68%	4.19%	4.06%	5.78%

#Returns are for the investment options listed for the periods stated ending on 30 June 2021. Returns are after fund taxes and investment expenses, but before account based fees.

*Past performance is not an indicator of future performance. Consider the Product Disclosure Statement and Target Market Determination on our website (www.unisuper.com.au) and your situation before making decisions, because we haven't. Issued by UniSuper Limited (ABN 54 006 027 121) as trustee of UniSuper (ABN 91 385 943 850).

CONTACT

Phone
1800 331 685

Email
enquiry@unisuper.com.au

SERVICE PROVIDERS

Administrator
UniSuper Management Pty Ltd

Asset consultant
Internal asset/investment management

Auditors
Internal: PricewaterhouseCoopers; External: Ernst & Young

Custodian
BNP Paribas Securities Services

Insurer
TAL Life Limited

Legal

UniSuper has a well resourced internal legal team specialising in superannuation law, investment transactions, litigation, dispute resolution and contract negotiation which is the principal source of legal advice to UniSuper. That advice is supplemented with advice from select external firms when required.

FUND VALUE
$1.1 billion

CONTACT

Phone
1300 658 422

Email
info@futuresuper.com.au

AT A GLANCE

USI 45 960 194 277 010

Year established 2014

Members 36,000

SERVICE PROVIDERS

Administrator
Iress

Asset consultant
Context Capital

Auditor
PWC

Custodian
Citi

Insurer
AIA Australia

Lawyers
DLA Piper

Future Super

www.futuresuper.com.au

Overview

Future Super exists to create a prosperous future free from climate change and inequality.

Investing is an opportunity cost. For every dollar in fossil fuels and other harmful industries, you miss a chance to invest in infrastructure and technology of the future.

We don't just invest responsibly and sustainably — we invest for impact.

Today, we build funds with zero exposure to fossil fuels and direct investments in clean energy projects.

Key features

- Negative screening for industries causing social or environmental harm (gambling, tobacco, armaments, fossil fuels, etc.)
- Investment in companies that are better performers on sustainable and ethical criteria (clean technology, IT, healthcare, renewables)
- Fully digital joining and ongoing member experience
- Active proxy voting and company engagement for positive environmental and social outcomes
- Baby Bump fee rebate for expecting and new parents
- No dollar-based administration fee for accounts under $6,000
- Easy opt-in insurance for members that need it
- Consistent competitive performance since inception for our investment options

Investment Performance	Growth Asset Weighting	1yr	3yrs (pa)	5yrs (pa)
Balanced Index	70%	13.87%	N/A	N/A
Balanced Impact	65%	12.56%	8.62%	7.72%
Renewables Plus Growth	75%	14.23%	9.51%	N/A
Balanced Growth Pension	70%	17.94%	11.58%	9.43%

Performance to 30 June 2021.

Hostplus Personal Super Plan

hostplus.com.au

HOSTPLUS

FUND VALUE
$66 billion

Overview
Hostplus is an award winning, quality super fund, recognised for consistent performance, low administration fees and exceptional service. And you can enjoy the rewards of membership right away, even if you don't work in the hospitality, tourism, recreation or sport industries. You can become a Hostplus member if you're self-employed or a full-time, part-time, temporary or casual employee and even if you're not in paid employment.

Key features
- Broad range of investment options.
- Run solely to benefit members.
- No commissions paid to financial advisers.
- Low administration fees of $1.50 per week.
- Affordable and flexible insurance options.
- Range of extra member benefits.

CONTACT

Phone
1300 467 875

Email
info@hostplus.com.au

At a glance
Spin HOS0100AU
Year established 1999
Members 1.3 million

---

superhero

superhero.com.au

superhero

FUND VALUE
New fund in 2021

Overview
Superhero Super is a superannuation fund that allows members to have a greater degree of control and transparency over their super without a self-managed super fund (SMSF). Superhero Super allows you to invest up to 75% of your super yourself directly into ASX 300 shares, listed investment companies (LICs) and exchange-traded funds (ETFs), without the costs and admin required with and SMSF.

Key features
- Invest your super directly into ASX300 shares & ETFs.
- Invest your super your way without an SMSF.
- Manage your super and trading investments in one place.
- Live market data and advanced investment order types.
- No commissions to financial advisors.
- Life and TPD insurance available.

CONTACT

Email
hello@superhero.com.au

At a glance
USI 43 905 581 638 018
Year established 2021
Members New fund in 2021

Personal Super Providers

Includes (a selection of corporate funds, Industry funds, Government funds and Corporate master trusts)

Advance Retirement Suite - Super Account	1800 819 935	advance.com.au
Agentia SuperSMA	1800 571 881	agentia.com.au
Allan Gray Superannuation	1300 604 604	onesuper.com/funds/allan-gray
AMG Personal Super	1300 264 264	amgsuper.com.au/products
AMIST Super Personal Division	1800 808 614	amist.com.au
AMP Flexible Lifetime Super	131 267	amp.com.au
AMP Flexible Super - Super Account	131 267	amp.com.au
AMP Super Directions - Personal Super Plan	131 737	amp.com.au
ANZ Australian Staff Superannuation Scheme - Personal Section	03 8654 7164	anzstaffsuper.com
ANZ OneAnswer Personal Super	133 665	anz.com.au
ANZ Smart Choice Super - Personal	131 287	anz.com.au
ANZ Super Advantage - Personal	133 863	anz.com.au
Aon Master Trust - Personal	1300 880 588	smartmonday.com.au
ARC Master Trust Personal	1300 209 088	arcmt.com.au
Asgard Elements Super Account	1800 998 185	asgard.com.au/products-and-services/elements
Asgard eWRAP Super Account	1800 998 185	asgard.com.au/products-and-services/eWRAP
Asgard Infinity eWrap Super Account	1800 731 812	asgard.com.au/products-and-services/infinity
Asgard Rollover Account	1800 998 185	asgard.com.au
Asgard Superannuation Account	1800 998 185	asgard.com.au
AssetChoice SuperWrap Essentials Personal Super Plan	1300 657 010	
AssetChoice SuperWrap Personal Super Plan	1300 657 010	
AssetLink SuperWrap Personal Super Plan	1300 657 010	
AustChoice Super Personal Division	1800 333 900	austchoice.com.au/super/product_information/Super_division
Australian Catholic Superannuation - Personal Plan	1300 658 776	catholicsuper.com.au
Australian Ethical Retail Superannuation Fund - Personal	1300 134 337	australianethical.com.au
Australian Practical Super	1300 862 862	onesuper.com/funds/australian-practical-superannuation
AustralianSuper Personal Plan	1300 300 273	australiansuper.com
AvSuper	1300 128 751	avsuper.com.au
AvWrap Retirement Service Super Division	1800 062 963	avwrap.com.au
Aware Super - Personal Retirement Plan	1800 620 305	aware.com.au
Aware Super - Tailored Super Plan	1800 620 305	aware.com.au
BEACON Superannuation Account	1800 555 744	beacongroup.com.au
Beacon Wrap Superannuation Service	1800 555 744	beaconwrap.com.au
Bendigo SmartStart Super - Personal	1800 033 426	sandhursttrustees.com.au/smartstart
BeyondBank Pension	13 25 85	beyondbank.com.au
BeyondBank Super	13 25 85	beyondbank.com.au

BT Lifetime Super Personal Plan	132 135	bt.com.au
BT Panorama Super	1300 881 716	bt.com.au
BT Personal Portfolio Service: Superannuation	132 135	westpac.com.au
BT Portfolio Administrator SuperWrap Personal Super Plan	1300 657 010	bt.com.au
BT Super for Life - Savings	1300 653 553	bt.com.au
BT SuperWrap Essentials Personal Super Plan	1300 657 010	bt.com.au
BT SuperWrap Personal Super Plan	1300 657 010	bt.com.au
BUSSQ Premium Choice	1300 773 776	bussq.com.au
CareSuper Personal Plan	1300 360 149	caresuper.com.au
Catholic Super Personal Plan	1300 550 273	csf.com.au
Cbus Personal Super	1300 361 784	cbussuper.com.au
Cbus Sole Traders Super	1300 361 784	cbussuper.com.au
Challenger Guaranteed Personal Superannuation		challenger.com.au/products/Superannuation
Christian Super - Personal	1300 360 907	christiansuper.com.au
ClearView Superannuation & Roll-overs	132 976	clearview.com.au/superannuation-investments-retirement/Superannuation
ClearView WealthFoundations Super	132 977	clearview.com.au/superannuation-investments-retirement/Superannuation
ClearView WealthSolutions Superannuation	1800 023 549	clearview.com.au/superannuation-investments-retirement/Superannuation
Club Plus Super Personal Division	1800 680 627	clubplussuper.com.au
Colonial First State - FirstChoice Personal Super	131 336	cfs.com.au
Colonial First State - FirstChoice Wholesale Personal Super	131 336	cfs.com.au
Colonial First State - FirstWrap Super	1300 769 619	cfs.com.au/firstwrap
Colonial First State Rollover & Superannuation Fund	131 336	cfs.com.au
Colonial PSL Personal Superannuation	1800 552 660	
Colonial Select Personal Superannuation	1800 552 660	
Colonial SuperChoice Personal Super	1800 805 898	
Complete Super 'Brightday'	1800 857 680	onesuper.com/funds/brightday
Crescent Wealth Superannuation Fund - Personal Division	1300 926 626	crescentwealth.com.au
Cruelty Free Superannuation Fund	1300 022 762	crueltyfreesuper.com.au
DIY Master Plan	1800 455 666	diymaster.com.au
East West Administration Service - Superannuation	1800 245 636	
EISS Super - Personal	1300 369 901	eisuper.com.au
Elevate Super	1800 875 148	elevatesuper.com.au
Enterprise Super - Personal	1800 816 575	
Equip MyFuture Personal	1800 682 626	equipsuper.com.au
Essential Super - Personal	134 074	commbank.com.au/super-retiring/essential-super
ESSSuper Accumulation Plan	1300 650 161	esssuper.com.au
eXpand Super	1800 517 124	myexpand.com.au
FairVine	02 8322 8199	fairvine.com.au
Fiducian Personal Superannuation	1800 653 263	fiducian.com.au/superannuation
First Super - Personal	1300 360 988	firstsuper.com.au
Freedom of Choice Superannuation	1800 806 013	freedomofchoice.com.au

Generations Personal Superannuation	1800 667 841	northonline.com.au/generations
GigSuper		gigsuper.com.au
GROW Super - Personal		onesuper.com/funds/grow
Grow Wrap Super Service	1800 094 423	wrapinvest.com.au
GuildSuper - Personal	1300 361 477	guildsuper.com.au
HUB24 Super	1300 854 994	hub24.com.au
ING DIRECT Living Super	133 464	ing.com.au/superannuation/living-super
Integra Super (Personal Division)	133 665	onepath.com.au/superandinvestment/integra-super
Intrust Super - Select Super	132 467	intrustsuper.com.au
IOOF Employer Super - Personal	1800 333 500	ioof.com.au
IOOF Portfolio Service Personal Superannuation	131 369	ioof.com.au
ipac iAccess Superannuation	1800 667 841	northonline.com.au/iaccess
Kogan Super	1800 517 212	kogansuper.com.au
legalsuper - Personal	1800 060 312	legalsuper.com.au
LifeTrack Personal Superannuation	1300 653 455	ioof.com.au
LUCRF Super Personal Plan	1300 130 780	lucrf.com.au
Macquarie Super Accumulator	1800 025 063	macquarie.com.au/advisers/solutions/macquarie-wrap
Macquarie Super Consolidator	1800 025 063	macquarie.com.au/advisers/solutions/macquarie-wrap
Macquarie Super Manager	1800 025 063	macquarie.com.au/advisers/solutions/macquarie-wrap
Macquarie SuperOptions Super Plan	1800 806 310	
MAP Super	1800 640 055	onesuper.com/funds/map-super
Mason Stevens Super Accumulation	1300 491 766	masonstevens.com.au
max Super Fund	1300 629 727	onesuper.com/funds/max-super
Media Super Personal	1800 640 886	mediasuper.com.au
Medical & Associated Professions Superannuation - Personal Division	1800 333 500	mapsuper.com.au
Mentor Superannuation Master Trust Superannuation & Rollovers	1300 550 899	mentorinvestments.com.au
Mercer Portfolio Services Superannuation Account	1800 998 010	mercerportfolioservice.com.au/cgi-bin/frameset.exe
MLC MasterKey Rollover	132 652	mlc.com.au
MLC MasterKey Super Fundamentals	132 652	mlc.com.au
MLC Navigator Access Super	132 652	mlc.com.au
MLC Navigator Retirement Plan - Superannuation Service	132 652	mlc.com.au
MLC Wrap Super - Super Service	132 652	mlc.com.au
MLC Wrap Super Series 2 - Super	132 652	mlc.com.au
mobiSuper	08 8223 1676	mobisuper.com.au
MyLife MySuper Personal Plan	1300 695 433	mylifemysuper.com.au
MyNorth Super	1800 667 841	northonline.com.au/mynorth-products/mynorth-super
MYONESUPER	1800 640 055	onesuper.com/funds/myonesuper
Nationwide Super Personal Division	1800 025 241	nationwidesuper.com.au
netwealth Super Accelerator Personal Super	1800 888 223	netwealth.com.au
NGS Super Accumulation Personal	1300 133 177	ngssuper.com.au
North Personal Superannuation	1800 667 841	northonline.com.au/other-products/north

Omniport Superannuation Service	1800 807 020	omniport.com.au
OneAnswer Frontier Personal Super	133 665	onepath.com.au
OneAnswer Personal Super	133 665	onepath.com.au
Optimix Superannuation	1800 060 710	onepath.com.au
Partnership Superannuation Plan	1800 819 499	asteron.com.au
Perpetual Select Super - Personal	1800 003 001	perpetual.com.au
Perpetual Super Wrap		perpetual.com.au
Perpetual WealthFocus Super Plan	1800 022 033	perpetual.com.au
Plum Personal Plan	1300 557 586	plum.com.au
PortfolioCare Elements Super Account	1800 646 234	amp.com.au
PortfolioCare eWrap Super Account	1800 646 234	amp.com.au
PortfolioCare Super Service Personal Account	1800 646 234	amp.com.au
Powerwrap Superannuation Account		powerwrap.com.au/products-services
Praemium SuperSMA		praemium.com/au
Premium Online Personal Super Plan	02 8253 2999	
premium super online	1800 025 063	
Prime Super - Personal (Health Division)	1800 675 839	primesuper.com.au
Prime Super - Personal (Prime Division)	1800 675 839	primesuper.com.au
Progress Super Fund - Personal	1300 880 736	
Pursuit Core Personal Superannuation	131 369	ioof.com.au
Pursuit Focus Personal Superannuation	1800 062 963	ioof.com.au
Pursuit Select Personal Superannuation	131 369	ioof.com.au
Qudos Super	1300 721 720	qudosbank.com.au/Products/WealthManagement/QudosSuper
Raiz Invest Super - Accumulation	1800 455 666	raizinvest.com.au
Resource Super General Division	1800 555 667	resourcesuper.com.au
RetireSelect	1800 640 055	onesuper.com/funds/retireselect
Russell iQ Super	1800 555 667	russell.com.au/super
Russell iQ Super Personal Division	1800 555 667	russellinvestments.com/au
smartMonday DIRECT	1300 880 588	smartmonday.com.au
Smartsave Personal Choice	1300 654 720	onesuper.com/funds/smartsave
Smartwrap Superannuation Account	03 8681 4600	powerwrap.com.au/products-services
Spaceship Super	1300 049 532	spaceship.com.au
Spirit Super Personal	1800 005 166	spiritsuper.com.au
StatewideSuper Personal	1300 651 865	statewide.com.au
Student Super Professional Super	1300 646 960	studentsuper.com.au
SUMMIT Master Trust Personal Super Plan	1800 667 841	northonline.com.au/summit
Suncorp Brighter Super personal	13 11 55	suncorp.com.au
Suncorp Everyday Super	13 11 55	suncorp.com.au
Super SA Flexible Rollover Product	1300 369 315	supersa.sa.gov.au/our_products/flexible_rollover_product
Superestate	1300 519 800	superestate.com.au
Symetry Active Super	08 8130 6600	symetry.com.au

Symetry Foundation Super	08 8130 6600	symetry.com.au
Symetry Lifetime Super	1800 880 219	symetry.com.au
Synergy Retirement Service - Superannuation	1800 245 636	
Telstra Super Personal Plus	1800 033 166	telstrasuper.com.au
The Emerald SuperWrap	1800 288 612	theemeraldwrap.com.au
The Employees Productivity Award Superannuation Trust	1800 814 005	
TW Super Division	1800 455 666	diymaster.com.au
Ventura Managed Account Portfolios Superannuation		venturafm.com.au/investment-management/managed-portfolios
Verve Super	1300 799 482	vervesuper.com.au
VicSuper FutureSaver - Personal	1300 366 216	vicsuper.com.au
Virgin Money Super Personal Division	1300 652 770	virginmoney.com.au/superannuation
Vision Personal Plan	1300 300 820	visionsuper.com.au
Voyage Superannuation Master Trust Superannuation & Rollovers	1800 892 353	wrapinvest.com.au/voyage
Wealth Manager SuperWrap Personal Super Plan	1300 657 010	
Wealth02 Super Simplifier - Super	1800 455 666	supersimplifier.com.au
Wealthtrac Superannuation Master Trust - Super Division	1300 552 447	wealthtrac.com.au
WealthView eWrap Super	1800 006 230	amp.com.au/wealthview
Westpac Lifetime Superannuation Service	131 817	westpac.com.au
Whole Super 'Super Prophets'	02 9024 6753	onesuper.com/funds/super-prophets
Xplore Super	1800 446 971	xplorewealth.com.au
YourChoice Super	1800 640 055	onesuper.com/funds/your-choice-super
Zurich Superannuation Plan	131 551	zurich.com.au/personal/superannuation/zurich-superannuation-plan

RETIREMENT INCOME PROVIDERS

Retirement funds are those funds that members join following their retirement. These funds can be associated with the fund they were a member of while working, e.g., they might be a sub-division, or they may be totally separate. The main difference for retirement funds is that they are designed to pay you a regular pension or "income stream" benefit, say each month, rather than help you accumulate new superannuation savings.

Aware Super

aware.com.au

Overview

Aware Super is a multi award-winning, profit-to-member industry fund that's been helping members with their superannuation, insurance, advice and retirement solutions for nearly 30 years. As *Money* magazine's 2021 Best Super Fund, Aware Super is recognised for consistent high performance, competitive fees while managing market fluctuations through our investment options.

As one of Australia's largest industry funds, managing $150 billion^ in savings for more than 1.1 million members. Aware Super's scale and skill enables them to adopt innovative, market leading investment strategies - helping members retire with more.

Aware Super has a strong heritage in providing superannuation for NSW and Victorian education, health, emergency services and public sector workers as well as local government workers in WA. Today, they are open to all Australian's and is a fund for community minded people who see no reason to sacrifice integrity for performance – doing well for themselves while doing good for all.

^as at August 2021

FUND VALUE
$150 billion

AT A GLANCE

SPIN FSS0100AU
Year established 1992
Members 1.1 million

Key features

- Profit to member fund operated solely for the benefit of members.
- Great value, with no entry or ongoing contribution fees, no withdrawal fee and no switching fee.
- A range of 12 investment options (including two socially responsible options) offering competitive returns. The Balanced Growth option (default) is ranked in the top ten for performance by Rainmaker Information for 5 and 10 year periods.
- All options have been divested of companies that manufacture cigarettes and tobacco products. All options will also be excluding direct investments in companies deriving 10% or more of their revenues directly from mining thermal or energy coal and companies deriving revenue from the manufacture and/or production of controversial weapons.*
- Transition to retirement and

retirement income stream products available.
- Variable pension income payment amounts and payment frequencies (subject to Government limits).
- Member information is readily available and accessible through a variety of channels, including online via our website or app, over the phone and face to face via our member service centres.
- All information is provided in plain English to help members understand their super.
- Full range of advice services from single issue phone advice at no additional fee, through to fee-based comprehensive advice provided by Aware Financial Services Australia Limited, ABN 86 003 742 756, AFSL 238430. Advice can include investment decisions, retirement income projections, estate planning and aged care services.

Extra benefits available

- Mobile website or app
- Newsletters for members
- Education and retirement seminars
- Online account access
- Investment flexibility
- Multi-manager-investment choice(s)
- Ethical/SRI investment choice(s)
- Online investment switching
- Monthly or quarterly investment reports
- Account flexibility
- Can join without an employer
- Explorer Tool: See how your super is tracking today and how much the retirement lifestyle you want could cost.
- Binding death benefit nominations

Financial Planning available

- Limited Advice
- Comprehensive Financial Planning

Fees	
Withdrawal fee	$0
Management Cost: member fee ($ per week/ annum)	$52 per year + 0.2% p.a. of account balance capped at $1,500 per year.
Management Cost: investment fee (% pa)	0.03% - 0.99%
Switching fee	$0
Other	$0

Investment Performance	Growth Asset Weighting	1yr	3yrs (pa)	5yrs (pa)	10yrs (pa)
Balanced Growth	49.30%	12.43%	6.94%	7.95%	7.94%
Conservative Growth	19.50%	4.49%	3.94%	4.65%	5.38%
Diversified Socially Responsible	48.60%	12.39%	6.89%	7.81%	8.12%
Growth	69.20%	18.83%	9.22%	10.38%	9.66%
High Growth	84.40%	23.84%	10.85%	12.33%	11.12%

Performance to 30 June 2021. Please note that all figures reflect net investment performance, i.e. net of investment tax, investment management fees and the maximum applicable ongoing management and membership fees.

* From 1 October 2020 all options will also be excluding direct investments in companies deriving 10% or more of their revenues directly from mining thermal or energy coal and companies deriving revenue from the manufacture and/or production of controversial weapons including chemical weapons, cluster munitions, land mines and depleted uranium. Due to liquidity constraints, it may take time to divest unlisted thermal coal mining assets and there may be a small residual exposure. Such assets will be sold at fair value as soon as reasonably practicable, but no later than 30 June 2023.

CONTACT

Phone
1300 650 873

Email
enquiries@aware.com.au

SERVICE PROVIDERS

Administrator
Mercer Administration Services (Australia)

Asset consultant
Willis Towers Watson

Auditors
Deloitte

Custodian
State Street Australia Limited

Hostplus Pension

hostplus.com.au

HOSTPLUS

FUND VALUE
$66 billion

Overview

A Hostplus Pension is a smart way to secure a regular income in retirement, or while you transition to retirement (TTR). With flexible payment options, a wide choice of investments and online access, you're in control of your retirement lifestyle at a low $4.50 a week administration fee.

At a glance

SPIN HOS0100AU
Year established 2009
Members 1.3 million

Key features

- Flexible payment frequency and income amounts (limits apply).
- Consistent long-term investment performance.
- Low administration fees of $4.50 per week.
- Freedom to choose your investment strategy.
- Offers Account-based pension and Transition to Retirement accounts.
- CPIplus investment option offers predetermined rate of return for a defined period.

CONTACT

Phone
1300 348 546

Email
pensions@hostplus.com.au

Retirement Income Providers

Includes (a selection of corporate funds, Industry funds, Government funds and Corporate master trusts)

Active Super Account-Based Pension Plan	1300 547 873	activesuper.com.au
Advance Retirement Suite - Pension Account	1800 819 935	advance.com.au
Allan Gray Retirement	1300 604 604	onesuper.com/funds/allan-gray
AMG Core Pension	1300 264 264	amgsuper.com.au/products
AMG Pension	1300 264 264	amgsuper.com.au/products
AMG Term Allocated Pension	1300 264 264	amgsuper.com.au/products
AMIST Pension	1800 255 521	amist.com.au
AMP Flexible Lifetime Allocated Pension	131 267	amp.com.au
AMP Flexible Lifetime Term Pension	131 267	amp.com.au
AMP Flexible Super - Retirement Account	131 267	amp.com.au
AMP Retirement Directions Allocated Pension Plan	133 056	amp.com.au
AMP SignatureSuper - Allocated Pension	1300 366 019	amp.com.au
ANZ Australian Staff Superannuation Scheme - Retirement Section	1800 000 086	anzstaffsuper.com
ANZ OneAnswer Pension	133 665	anz.com.au
ANZ OneAnswer Term Allocated Pension	133 665	anz.com.au
ANZ Smart Choice Pension	131 287	anz.com.au
ANZ Super Advantage - Allocated Pension	133 863	anz.com.au
Aon Master Trust - Pension	1300 880 588	smartmonday.com.au
Asgard Allocated Pension Account	1800 998 185	asgard.com.au
Asgard Elements Allocated Pension Account	1800 998 185	asgard.com.au/products-and-services/elements
Asgard Elements Term Allocated Pension Account	1800 998 185	asgard.com.au/products-and-services/elements
Asgard eWRAP Allocated Pension Account	1800 998 185	asgard.com.au/products-and-services/eWRAP
Asgard eWRAP Term Allocated Pension Account	1800 988 185	asgard.com.au/products-and-services/eWRAP
Asgard Infinity eWrap Pension Account	1800 731 812	asgard.com.au/products-and-services/infinity
AssetChoice SuperWrap Essentials Pension Plan	1300 657 010	
AssetChoice SuperWrap Essentials Term Allocated Pension Plan	1300 657 010	
AssetChoice SuperWrap Pension Plan	1300 657 010	
AssetChoice SuperWrap Term Allocated Pension Plan	1300 657 010	
AssetLink SuperWrap Pension Plan	1300 657 010	
AssetLink SuperWrap Term Allocated Pension Plan	1300 657 010	
AustChoice Super Account-Based Pension	1800 333 900	austchoice.com.au/super/product_information/pension_division
AustChoice Super Term Allocated Pension	1800 333 900	austchoice.com.au/super/product_information/pension_division
Australia Post Superannuation Scheme - Pension	1300 360 373	apss.com.au
Australian Catholic Superannuation - RetireChoice	1300 658 776	catholicsuper.com.au
Australian Catholic Superannuation - RetireSmart	1300 658 776	catholicsuper.com.au
Australian Ethical Retail Superannuation Fund - Pension	1300 134 337	australianethical.com.au

Australian Practical Pension	1300 862 862	onesuper.com/funds/australian-practical-superannuation
AustralianSuper Choice Income	1300 789 932	australiansuper.com
AvSuper Retirement Income Stream	1800 805 088	avsuper.com.au
AvWrap Retirement Service Pension Division	1800 062 963	avwrap.com.au
AvWrap Retirement Service Term Allocated Pension	1800 062 963	avwrap.com.au
Aware Super - Allocated Pension Fund	1800 620 305	aware.com.au
Aware Super - Flexible Income Plan	1800 620 305	aware.com.au
Aware Super - Term Allocated Pension	1800 620 305	aware.com.au
BEACON Allocated Pension Account	1800 555 744	beacongroup.com.au
BEACON Term Allocated Pension Account	1800 555 744	beacongroup.com.au
Beacon Wrap Allocated Pension Service	1800 555 744	beaconwrap.com.au
Beacon Wrap Term Allocated Pension Service	1800 555 744	beaconwrap.com.au
Bendigo SmartStart Pension	1800 033 426	sandhursttrustees.com.au/smartstart
BT Lifetime Flexible Pension	132 135	bt.com.au/personal/superannuation
BT Personal Portfolio Service: Allocated Pension	132 135	westpac.com.au
BT Portfolio Administrator SuperWrap Pension Plan	1300 657 010	bt.com.au
BT Super for Life - Retirement	1300 653 553	bt.com.au/personal/superannuation/solutions/bt-super-for-life
BT SuperWrap Essentials Pension Plan	1300 657 010	bt.com.au
BT SuperWrap Essentials Term Allocated Pension Plan	1300 657 010	bt.com.au
BT SuperWrap Pension Plan	1300 657 010	bt.com.au
BT SuperWrap Term Allocated Pension Plan	1300 657 010	bt.com.au
BUSSQ Income Account	1800 736 746	bussq.com.au
BUSSQ Term Allocated Pension	1800 657 216	bussq.com.au
CareSuper Pension	1300 360 149	caresuper.com.au
Catholic Super Term Allocated Pension	1300 550 273	csf.com.au
Cbus Super Income Stream	1300 361 784	cbussuper.com.au
Challenger Guaranteed Allocated Pension		challenger.com.au/products/Superannuation
Christian Super - Term Allocated Pension	1800 451 566	christiansuper.com.au
Christian Super Pension	1800 451 566	christiansuper.com.au
ClearView Pension Plan	132 976	clearview.com.au/superannuation-investments-retirement/Retirement
ClearView WealthFoundations Pension	132 977	clearview.com.au/superannuation-investments-retirement/Retirement
ClearView WeatlhSolutions Retirement Income	1800 023 549	clearview.com.au/superannuation-investments-retirement/Retirement
Club Plus Pension	1800 204 194	www.clubplussuper.com.au
Colonial First State - FirstChoice Pension	131 336	cfs.com.au
Colonial First State - FirstChoice Term Allocated Pension	131 336	cfs.com.au
Colonial First State - FirstChoice Wholesale Pension	131 336	cfs.com.au
Colonial First State - FirstChoice Wholesale Term Allocated Pension	131 336	cfs.com.au
Colonial First State - FirstWrap Pension	1300 769 619	cfs.com.au/firstwrap
Colonial First State - FirstWrap Term Allocated Pension	1300 769 619	cfs.com.au/firstwrap
Colonial PSL Master Fund Allocated Pension	1800 552 660	
Colonial Select Allocated Pension Plan	1800 552 660	

Commonwealth Bank Group Super - Retirement Access	1800 023 928	oursuperfund.com.au
Commonwealth PensionSelect	132 221	commbank.com.au
Complete Super 'Brightday' Pension	1800 857 680	onesuper.com/funds/brightday
CSC retirement income	1300 736 096	csc.gov.au
DIY Master Plan (Pension)	1800 455 666	diymaster.com.au
East West Administration Service - Allocated Pension	1800 245 636	
EISS Pension	1300 369 901	eisuper.com.au
Electricity Industry Superannuation Scheme - Income Stream	1300 307 844	electricsuper.com.au
Energy Super Income Stream	1300 363 240	energysuper.com.au
Enterprise Super - Pension	1800 816 575	
Equip MyPension	1800 682 626	equipsuper.com.au
Equip Pensions	1800 682 626	equipsuper.com.au
ESSSuper Income Streams	1300 650 161	esssuper.com.au
eXpand Pension	1800 517 124	myexpand.com.au
Fiducian Account Based Pension	1800 653 263	fiducian.com.au/superannuation
Fiducian Term Allocated Pension	1800 653 263	fiducian.com.au/superannuation
Fire and Emergency Services Superannuation Fund - Pension	08 9382 8444	fessuper.com.au
First Super - Allocated Pensions	1300 360 988	firstsuper.com.au
Freedom of Choice Pension	1800 806 013	freedomofchoice.com.au
Future Super Pension Plan	1300 658 422	futuresuper.com.au
Generations Personal Pension	1800 667 841	northonline.com.au/generations
GESB Retirement Income Allocated Pension	13 43 72	gesb.com.au
GESB Retirement Income Term Allocated Pension	134 372	gesb.com.au
Grow Wrap Pension Service	1800 094 423	wrapinvest.com.au
GuildPension	1300 665 722	guildsuper.com.au/pension
HUB24 Super - Pension	1300 854 994	hub24.com.au
ING DIRECT Living Super - Pension Account	133 464	ing.com.au/superannuation/living-super
Integra Allocated Pension	133 665	onepath.com.au/superandinvestment/integra-super
Intrust Super - Super Stream	132 467	intrustsuper.com.au
IOOF Employer Super - Pension	1800 333 500	ioof.com.au
IOOF Portfolio Service Allocated Pension	131 369	ioof.com.au
IOOF Portfolio Service Term Allocated Pension	1800 062 963	ioof.com.au
ipac iAccess Allocated Pension	1800 667 841	northonline.com.au/iaccess
Labour Union Co-operative Retirement Fund - Term Allocated Pension	1300 130 780	lucrf.com.au
legalsuper - Pension	1800 060 312	legalsuper.com.au
LESF and Macmahon Super - Pension	1800 359 686	onesuper.com/funds/lesf-macmahon-super
LGIAsuper Pension	1800 444 396	lgiasuper.com.au
LifeTrack Cashback Pension	1300 653 455	ioof.com.au
Local Government Superannuation Scheme (QLD) - Term Allocated Pension	1800 444 396	lgiasuper.com.au
LUCRF Pensions	1300 130 780	lucrf.com.au
Lutheran Super - Pension	1800 635 796	lutheransuper.com.au

Macquarie Pension Consolidator	1800 025 063	macquarie.com.au/advisers/solutions/macquarie-wrap
Macquarie Pension Manager	1800 025 063	macquarie.com.au/advisers/solutions/macquarie-wrap
Macquarie SuperOptions Pension Plan	1800 808 001	
Macquarie SuperOptions Term Allocated Pension Plan	1800 808 001	
Macquarie Term Allocated Pension Manager	1800 025 063	
MAP Pension	1800 640 055	onesuper.com/funds/map-super
MAP Term Allocated Pension Plan	1800 640 055	onesuper.com/funds/map-super
Maritime Super Allocated Pension	1800 757 607	maritimesuper.com.au
Mason Stevens Super Pension	1300 491 766	masonstevens.com.au
max Super Fund - Pension	1300 629 727	onesuper.com/funds/max-super
Meat Industry Employees' Superannuation Fund - Pension	1800 252 099	miesf.com.au
Media Super Retirement Pension	1800 640 886	mediasuper.com.au
Medical & Associated Professions Pension	1800 333 500	mapsuper.com.au
Mercer Portfolio Services Allocated Pension	1800 998 010	mercerportfolioservice.com.au/cgi-bin/frameset.exe
Mercer Portfolio Services Term Allocated Pension	1800 998 010	mercerportfolioservice.com.au/cgi-bin/frameset.exe
Mercer Super Trust - Allocated Pension Division	1800 633 403	mercerfinancialservices.com
Mercy Super Income Streams	1300 368 891	mercysuper.com.au
Mine Super Account-based Pension	13 64 63	mine.com.au
Mine Super Term Allocated Pension	1300 287 262	auscoalsuper.com.au
MLC MasterKey Pension Fundamentals	132 652	mlc.com.au
MLC MasterKey Term Allocated Pension	132 652	mlc.com.au
MLC Navigator Access Pension	132 652	mlc.com.au
MLC Navigator Retirement Plan - Pension Service	132 652	mlc.com.au
MLC Navigator Retirement Plan Series 2 - Pension Service	132 652	mlc.com.au
MLC Wrap Super - Pension Service	132 652	mlc.com.au
MLC Wrap Super Series 2 - Pension	132 652	mlc.com.au
MLC Wrap Term Allocated Pension	132 652	mlc.com.au
MyLife MyPension	1300 550 273	mylifemypension.com.au
MyNorth Pension	1800 667 841	northonline.com.au/mynorth-products/mynorth-pension
MYONESUPER Pension	1800 640 055	onesuper.com/funds/myonesuper
NESS Pension	1800 022 067	nesssuper.com.au
netwealth Super Accelerator Standard Income Stream	1800 888 223	netwealth.com.au
netwealth Super Accelerator Term Allocated Pension	1800 888 223	netwealth.com.au
NGS Super Income	1300 133 177	ngssuper.com.au
North Personal Pension	1800 667 841	northonline.com.au/other-products/north
Omniport Pension Service - Allocated Pension	1800 807 020	omniport.com.au
Omniport Pension Service - Term Allocated Pension	1800 807 020	omniport.com.au
OneAnswer Frontier Pension	133 665	onepath.com.au
OneAnswer Pension	133 665	onepath.com.au
OneAnswer Term Allocated Pension	133 665	onepath.com.au
Optimix Allocated Pension	1800 060 710	onepath.com.au

Optimix Term Allocated Pension	1800 060 710	optimix.com.au
Optimum Allocated Annuity	1800 819 499	asteron.com.au
Partnership Allocated Pension Plan	1800 819 499	asteron.com.au
Perpetual Pension Wrap		perpetual.com.au
Perpetual Select Pension Plan	1800 003 001	perpetual.com.au
Perpetual Select Super - Term Allocated Pension	1800 003 001	perpetual.com.au
Perpetual WealthFocus Pension Plan	1800 022 033	perpetual.com.au
Perpetual WealthFocus Term Allocated Pension Plan	1800 022 033	perpetual.com.au
Personal Choice Retirement Plan - Allocated Pension	1800 245 636	
Plum Retirement Income	1300 557 586	plum.com.au
PortfolioCare Allocated Pension Service	1800 646 234	amp.com.au
PortfolioCare Elements Allocated Pension Account	1800 646 234	amp.com.au
PortfolioCare Elements Term Allocated Pension	1800 646 234	amp.com.au
PortfolioCare eWrap Allocated Pension Account	1800 646 234	amp.com.au
PortfolioCare eWrap Term Allocated Pension	1800 646 234	amp.com.au
PortfolioCare Term Allocated Pension	1800 646 234	amp.com.au
PortfolioOne Term Allocated Pension	1800 005 043	portfolioone.openportal.com.au/portal/portfolioone
Powerwrap Pension Account		powerwrap.com.au/products-services
Praemium SuperSMA Pension		praemium.com/au
Premium Online Allocated Pension	02 8253 2999	
premium pension online	1800 025 063	
Prime Super - Income Stream	1800 675 839	primesuper.com.au
Progress Super Fund - Pension Plan	1300 880 736	
Pursuit Core Allocated Pension	131 369	ioof.com.au
Pursuit Core Term Allocated Pension	131 369	ioof.com.au
Pursuit Focus Allocated Pension	1800 062 963	ioof.com.au
Pursuit Select Allocated Pension	131 369	ioof.com.au
Pursuit Select Term Allocated Pension	131 369	ioof.com.au
Qantas Superannuation Plan - Gateway Income Account	1300 362 967	qantassuper.com.au
QSuper Income Account	1300 360 750	qsuper.qld.gov.au
Qudos Pension	1300 721 720	qudosbank.com.au/Products/WealthManagement/QudosSuper
Raiz Invest Super - Pension	1800 455 666	raizinvest.com.au
REI Super Pension	1300 134 433	reisuper.com.au
Rest Pension	1300 305 778	rest.com.au/member/products/rest-pension
REST Term Allocated Pension	1300 305 778	rest.com.au
RetireSelect - Pension	1800 640 055	onesuper.com/funds/retireselect
Russell iQ Retirement	1800 300 353	russell.com.au/retirement
Russell Term Allocated Pension Division	1800 555 667	russellinvestments.com/au
smartMonday PENSION	1300 112 403	smartmonday.com.au
smartMonday PENSION TESF	1300 880 588	smartmonday.com.au
Smartsave - Smart Pensions	1300 654 720	onesuper.com/funds/smartsave

Smartsave Term Allocated Pension	1300 654 720	onesuper.com/funds/smartsave
Spectrum Super Term Allocated Pension Division	1800 333 500	
Spirit Super Pension	1800 005 166	spiritsuper.com.au
Spirit Super Term Allocated Pension	1800 005 166	spiritsuper.com.au
StatewideSuper Pension	1300 651 865	statewide.com.au
SUMMIT Master Trust Personal Pension Plan - Allocated Pension	1800 667 841	northonline.com.au/summit
SUMMIT Master Trust Personal Pension Plan - Term Allocated Pension	1800 667 841	northonline.com.au/summit
Suncorp Brighter Super pension	13 11 55	suncorp.com.au
Suncorp Everyday Super Pension	13 11 55	suncorp.com.au
Sunsuper for Life - Income Account	131 184	sunsuper.com.au
Super SA Income Stream	1300 369 315	supersa.sa.gov.au/our_products/income_stream
Symetry Active Pension	08 8130 6600	symetry.com.au
Symetry Allocated Pension	1800 880 219	symetry.com.au
Symetry Foundation Pension	08 8130 6600	symetry.com.au
Symetry Term Allocated Pension	1800 880 219	symetry.com.au
Synergy Retirement Service - Allocated Pension	1800 245 636	
Telstra Super RetireAccess	1800 033 166	telstrasuper.com.au
Telstra Super RetireAccess Term Allocated Pension	1800 033 166	telstrasuper.com.au
The Emerald PensionWrap	1800 288 612	theemeraldwrap.com.au
TransPension	1800 222 071	twusuper.com.au
UniSuper - Defined Benefit Indexed Pension Division	1800 331 685	unisuper.com.au
UniSuper Pension	1800 331 685	unisuper.com.au
VicSuper Flexible Income	1300 366 216	vicsuper.com.au
VicSuper Term Allocated Pension	1300 366 216	vicsuper.com.au
Vision Income Streams	1300 017 589	visionsuper.com.au
Vision Super - Term Allocated Pension	1300 017 589	visionsuper.com.au
VISSF Pension	1300 660 027	vissf.com.au
Voyage Superannuation Master Trust Allocated Pension	1800 892 353	wrapinvest.com.au/voyage
Voyage Superannuation Master Trust Term Allocated Pension	1800 892 353	wrapinvest.com.au/voyage
Wealth Manager SuperWrap Pension Plan	1300 657 010	
WealthO2 Super Simplifier - Pension	1800 455 666	supersimplifier.com.au
Wealthtrac Superannuation Master Trust - Pension Division	1300 552 477	wealthtrac.com.au
Wealthtrac Superannuation Master Trust Term Allocated Pension	1800 893 091	wrapinvest.com.au/wealthtrac
WealthView eWrap Allocated Pension	1800 006 230	amp.com.au/wealthview
WealthView eWrap Term Allocated Pension	1800 006 230	amp.com.au/wealthview
Whole Super 'Super Prophets' - Pension	02 9024 6753	onesuper.com/funds/super-prophets
Xplore Pension	1800 446 971	xplorewealth.com.au
YourChoice Super - Pension	1800 640 055	onesuper.com/funds/your-choice-super
Zurich Account-Based Pension	131 551	zurich.com.au/personal/superannuation/zurich-account-based-pension
Zurich Term Allocated Pension	131 551	zurich.com.au

FUND INDEX

An A-Z listing of Australia's providers, including workplace super providers, personal super providers and retirement income providers.

INDEX

INDEX

INDEX

UniSuper	Workplace super providers	118
UniSuper - Defined Benefit Division	Workplace super providers	114
UniSuper - Defined Benefit Indexed Pension Division	Retirement super products	136
UniSuper Pension	Retirement super products	136
UniSuper Personal Accounts	Personal super providers	118
Ventura Managed Account Portfolios Superannuation	Personal super providers	126
Verve Super	Personal super providers	126
VicSuper Flexible Income	Retirement super products	136
VicSuper FutureSaver	Workplace super providers	114
VicSuper FutureSaver - Personal	Personal super providers	126
VicSuper Term Allocated Pension	Retirement super products	136
Virgin Money Super Employer Division	Workplace super providers	114
Virgin Money Super Personal Division	Personal super providers	126
Vision Income Streams	Retirement super products	136
Vision Personal Plan	Personal super providers	126
Vision Super - Defined Benefit	Workplace super providers	114
Vision Super - Term Allocated Pension	Retirement super products	136
Vision Super Saver	Workplace super providers	114
VISSF Accumulation	Workplace super providers	114
VISSF Pension	Retirement super products	136
Voyage Superannuation Master Trust Allocated Pension	Retirement super products	136
Voyage Superannuation Master Trust Superannuation & Rollovers	Personal super providers	126
Voyage Superannuation Master Trust Term Allocated Pension	Retirement super products	136
Wealth Manager SuperWrap Pension Plan	Retirement super products	136
Wealth Manager SuperWrap Personal Super Plan	Personal super providers	126
WealthO2 Super Simplifier - Pension	Retirement super products	136
WealthO2 Super Simplifier - Super	Personal super providers	126
Wealthtrac Superannuation Master Trust - Pension Division	Retirement super products	136
Wealthtrac Superannuation Master Trust - Super Division	Personal super providers	126
Wealthtrac Superannuation Master Trust Term Allocated Pension	Retirement super products	136
WealthView eWrap Allocated Pension	Retirement super products	136
WealthView eWrap Super	Personal super providers	126
WealthView eWrap Term Allocated Pension	Retirement super products	136
Westpac Lifetime Superannuation Service	Personal super providers	126
Whole Super 'Super Prophets'	Personal super providers	126
Whole Super 'Super Prophets' - Pension	Retirement super products	136
Xplore Pension	Retirement super products	136
Xplore Super	Personal super providers	126
YourChoice Super	Personal super providers	126
YourChoice Super - Pension	Retirement super products	136
Zurich Account-Based Pension	Retirement super products	136
Zurich Superannuation Plan	Personal super providers	126
Zurich Term Allocated Pension	Retirement super products	136